Ingrid Jonker

OHIO SHORT HISTORIES OF AFRICA

This series of Ohio Short Histories of Africa is meant for those who are looking for a brief but lively introduction to a wide range of topics in South African history, politics, and biography, written by some of the leading experts in their fields.

Steve Biko
by Lindy Wilson
ISBN: 978-0-8214-2025-6
e-ISBN: 978-0-8214-4441-2

Spear of the Nation (Umkhonto weSizwe):
South Africa's Liberation Army, 1960s–1990s
by Janet Cherry
ISBN: 978-0-8214-2026-3
e-ISBN: 978-0-8214-4443-6

Epidemics:
The Story of South Africa's Five Most Lethal Human Diseases
by Howard Phillips
ISBN: 978-0-8214-2028-7
e-ISBN: 978-0-8214-4442-9

South Africa's Struggle for Human Rights
by Saul Dubow
ISBN: 978-0-8214-2027-0
e-ISBN: 978-0-8214-4440-5

San Rock Art
by J. D. Lewis-Williams
ISBN: 978-0-8214-2045-4
e-ISBN: 978-0-8214-4458-0

Ingrid Jonker:
Poet under Apartheid
by Louise Viljoen
ISBN: 978-0-8214-2048-5
e-ISBN: 978-0-8214-4460-3

Ingrid Jonker
Poet under Apartheid

Louise Viljoen

OHIO UNIVERSITY PRESS

ATHENS

Ohio University Press, Athens, Ohio 45701
www.ohioswallow.com
All rights reserved

First published by Jacana Media (Pty) Ltd in 2012
10 Orange Street
Sunnyside
Auckland Park 2092
South Africa
(+27 11) 628-3200
www.jacana.co.za

© Louise Viljoen, 2012

First published in North America in 2013 by Ohio University Press
Printed in the United States of America
Ohio University Press books are printed on acid-free paper ⊗ ™

20 19 18 17 16 15 14 13   5 4 3 2 1

ISBN: 978-0-8214-2048-5
e-ISBN: 978-0-8214-4460-3

Library of Congress Cataloging-in-Publication Data
Viljoen, Louise.
  Ingrid Jonker : poet under apartheid / Louise Viljoen.
      pages cm. — (Ohio Short Histories of Africa)
  Includes bibliographical references and index.
  ISBN 978-0-8214-2048-5 (pb : acid-free paper) — ISBN
978-0-8214-4460-3 (electronic)
  1. Jonker, Ingrid, 1933–1965. 2. Authors, Afrikaans—20th century—
Biography. I. Title.
  PT6592.2.O5Z93 2013
  839.3'614—dc23
  [B]
                                2013001102

Cover design by Sebastian Biot

Contents

Acknowledgements

I gratefully acknowledge the help of the following people in writing this book:

Petrovna Metelerkamp for giving freely of information and advice;

Ann Torlesse and Cecilia Blight for their help in accessing material about Ingrid Jonker at NELM;

NELM for permission to reproduce photographs and literary materials held by them in the Cope Collection;

Lynne Fourie and Marina Brink for their help in accessing material about Ingrid Jonker in the Stellenbosch University Library;

Michael Cope for giving permission to quote from his father's papers;

The Ingrid Jonker Trust for permission to quote from Ingrid Jonker's poems and for the use of photographs;

André Brink and Antjie Krog for kind permission to

use their translations of some of Ingrid Jonker's poems from their collection entitled *Black Butterflies* (Cape Town, 2007);

Breyten Breytenbach for permission to quote from his poem 'Ballade van ontroue bemindes';

André Brink for talking to me about Ingrid Jonker;

Gerhard Geldenhuys for information about documents regarding Abraham and Ingrid Jonker in the Western Cape Archives and Office of the Master of the Supreme Court, Cape Town;

Joan-Mari Barendse for invaluable research assistance;

Chris van der Merwe for comments on and advice about the text;

Russell Martin for the careful editing of the text.

Every effort has been made to identify the copyright holders of the photographs reproduced in this book. Should there be any errors or omissions, we shall gladly rectify them in the next impression.

Louise Viljoen
2012

1

Writing Ingrid Jonker

> *'There can never be a definitive biography,*
> *merely a version, an attempt, an essay which in*
> *time reveals how completely all such attempts*
> *bear the impress of the age in which it was*
> *written.'*
>
> — *Eric Homberger & John Charmley,*
> The troubled face of biography

The fascination with Ingrid Jonker

When Ingrid Jonker took her own life by walking into the sea at Three Anchor Bay in Cape Town on 19 July 1965 at the age of 31, she became the stuff of legend and rumour. Looking back on her legacy, one may wonder why this is so. The shortness of her life and the slenderness of her literary oeuvre seem out of all proportion to the biographical, critical and creative attention that has been devoted to her. Her collected writings can be contained within one compact volume. Apart from two volumes of poetry published in her lifetime and a volume published posthumously, she left only a few short stories, a play and a scattering of other texts.

To what should one ascribe her iconic status and the continuing fascination with her life and work? The answer to this probably lies in a combination of factors. There is no doubt that the easily sensationalised details of her life provide a provocative glimpse into a particularly turbulent period of Afrikaner and South African history. Her private history (a materially deprived childhood, a difficult relationship with her father, her frank and spontaneous sexuality, her unhappy love affairs, her suicide) coincided with major developments in public history. The 1950s saw a rapid escalation of apartheid laws to ensure the segregation of South African society and the early 1960s began dramatically with the shootings at Sharpeville, the banning of the ANC and PAC, South Africa's withdrawal from the Commonwealth and the declaration of a Republic. Ingrid's response to these and other events and her identification with the plight of the oppressed in South Africa brought her into conflict with her father, at that time a National Party politician, as well as with other authority figures of Afrikanerdom. As part of a bohemian circle of friends with liberal values in Cape Town, she identified herself with the ideal of a society in which freedom of speech and association was recognised. Her life was also closely intertwined with the work of the Sestigers, who were busy rewriting Afrikaner history and literature by opposing the political and literary establishment of the time.

Although hers was an eventful life that provides a win-

10

dow on the tensions of South Africa at a certain moment in its history, it would not have made the same impact but for her poetry. For her mentor, Uys Krige, her poetry was 'the essential Ingrid stripped of her incompleteness, of the little human flaws and shortcomings we all share'.[1] An academic analysis of her poetry's appeal would refer to its pure lyricism, its powerful almost surrealist imagery, its confident musicality, its sensitivity to all the nuances of her mother tongue and its ability to infuse the political with the personal. It is more difficult to discern why her best poems appeal to both poetry-lovers and poetry-avoiders alike. One of the answers may lie in the fact that she started writing poems when she was about six and her poetry, despite its increasing sophistication, never lost its almost childlike clarity and freshness. It may also be that readers feel the force of her urgency to communicate with others through her poetry, that they feel directly spoken to by her poems.

It is therefore not surprising that it was her poetry, more specifically the poem 'Die kind' (translated into English as 'The child'), that brought her to the attention of South Africa and the larger world when Nelson Mandela read it at the opening of South Africa's first democratic parliament on 24 May 1994. Without doubt, Mandela's reference to Ingrid Jonker contributed hugely to the revival of interest in her person and her work. Although she always had a strong following in Afrikaans literary circles,[2] journalists started digging up the details of her life in the week after Mandela's speech and a new revised edition of her collected works was published before the year was out. In the years that followed new English translations of her work appeared and several documentary films were produced. The first biographical works about her life also started to see the light. A short and gripping biography by the Dutch novelist Henk van Woerden was included in *Ik herhaal je* (2000), a volume that included Gerrit Komrij's translations of Jonker's poetry into Dutch. The first attempt at a comprehensive overview of her life was Petrovna Metelerkamp's *Ingrid Jonker: Beeld van 'n digterslewe* (2003). Rather than a conventional biography, this impressive book consisted of a collection of documents about Ingrid Jonker's life, with the hand of the biographer only visible in the selection and ordering of the material as well as in short interlinking pieces. More information about Ingrid Jonker's life came to light in 2006 when the clinical psychologist L.M. van der Merwe published a series of interviews conducted with people who were close to her for his doctoral thesis in psychology twelve years after her death, in *Gesprekke oor Ingrid Jonker* [Conversations about Ingrid Jonker]. In addition to two Afrikaans plays about her life – *Ingrid Jonker: Opdrag* (created by Jana Cilliers in cooperation with the writer Ryk Hattingh in 1997) and *Altyd Jonker* (written and produced by Saartjie Botha in 2006) – her life was captured in the 2011 film *Black Butterflies* by the Dutch director Paula van der Oest, starring Carice van Houten as Ingrid Jonker.

Such is the fascination with Ingrid Jonker that André Brink has spoken of an 'industry' that has sprung up around her death.[3] It is a fascination that shows no sign of abating.

Writing Ingrid Jonker

In using the materials available to reconstruct Ingrid Jonker's life and interpret her work, we must remember that no document is inert or innocent. Letters, diaries, and biographical and autobiographical writings are never neutral representations of reality. They often constitute deliberate acts of self-creation, self-justification or even self-promotion that have to be reckoned with. Moreover, private documents often make use of rhetorical strategies or coded languages that are difficult to interpret. For the biographer, therefore, the task at hand is not simply a matter of decoding the available documents, but rather of cautiously interpreting them. The same goes for information gleaned from interviews conducted with people who knew Ingrid Jonker. Their memories are necessarily determined by the nature of their relationship with her and by their subjective interpretation of events. We also know that memories of the past are subject to complex processes of editing and erasure; nor are they free of self-interest and self-preservation. One could argue that the many photographs of Ingrid Jonker speak unambiguously to the viewer, that they are impervious to the passage of time and the erosion of memory. We should, however, heed Susan Sontag's warning that 'photography makes us feel that the world is more available than it really is'.[4] Photographs do not escape the mediatedness that the use of language inevitably entails.

Any biographical endeavour is also fraught with ethical questions. When reading documents like letters and diaries, it is difficult for the biographer to escape the feeling that she is invading another's private space. When writing about someone's private life and intimate thoughts, it is almost inevitable that the biographer should wonder what the limits of such revelations are. It is precisely this aspect of biography that has led critics to use the tropes of thievery, voyeurism, invasion and violation. On the other hand the right to privacy is not self-evident. Paul John Eakin observes in 'Mapping the ethics of life writing': 'Because we live our lives in relation to others, our privacies are largely shared, making it hard to demarcate where one life leaves off and another begins.' For Eakin, life writing, indeed life itself, is messier than traditional ethical models suggest. As he says, it is not easy to argue that one owns the facts of one's life, as Ted Hughes claimed in the face of the relentless biographers of his wife Sylvia Plath. Eakin identifies respect for the autobiographical subject as *the* basic guideline when writing either a biography or an autobiography.[5]

This will be an important guideline in my own attempt to reconstruct Ingrid Jonker's life and evaluate her work. For this reason I will not attempt to describe those parts of her life for which we have no information (a strategy perfectly acceptable in a novelised life). This brief introduction to her life and work, set against the background of her time and place, will also try to resist the temptation to romanticise a life lived in difficult circumstances or read it in terms of a single grand narrative that predetermined all the events in her life, be it political or psychoanalytical. Although I will discuss some of her literary texts and speculate about the connection between the writer's life and her writings, my attempts will be guided by the understanding that poems and stories originate from a complex interplay between fact and fiction and are sometimes pure fiction. This biography will engage with those details available in order to arrive at yet another understanding of the phenomenon Ingrid Jonker. It also builds on the work of those who have come before, thus taking its place as one of an ongoing series of interpretations of her life which will become more nuanced as further information becomes available. As such it is, inevitably, part of the 'industry' around Jonker.

2

Childhood and youth, 1933–1951

The child in me died quietly
neglected, blind and quite unspoilt.
– Ingrid Jonker, 'Puberty' from Black butterflies

The beginning

The beginning was inauspicious. Ingrid Jonker was born on 19 September 1933 on a farm near Douglas in the Northern Cape where her mother Beatrice was staying with her parents, Fanie and Annie Cilliers. Beatrice had left her husband Abraham Jonker when he accused her of carrying a child that was not his. Neighbours in the Cape Town suburb of Vredehoek where the Jonkers lived told of marital tensions and frequent arguments between Abraham and his wife, after which she often fled the house with her firstborn, Anna.[6] Beatrice's hurt at her husband's accusations must have run deep. A letter, dated 16 November 1933, shows her firmly rejecting Abraham's plea that she return to him.[7] The early 1930s were difficult times in South Africa. The economic depression as well as a severe drought brought great financial hardship, unemployment and poverty for many people. Although Ingrid's grandfather Fanie had been a relatively prosperous farmer in the Boland, he also fell on hard times. A memoir by his son, the physicist A.C. (Andries) Cilliers, tells us that Ingrid's grandfather bought a farm in the Douglas district, in all probability the one where Ingrid was born, in partnership with two of his sons in 1926. But depression and drought as well as the financial burden of caring for their divorced sister Beatrice and her two children forced them to sell the farm at a loss by 1934.[8] Thereafter, the small extended family, consisting of grandparents Fanie and Annie, daughter Beatrice and granddaughters Anna and Ingrid, lived on a succession of farms in the region[9] before moving to Durbanville, then still a village on the outskirts of Cape Town, in 1937.

Durbanville

Ingrid spent her childhood years in a succession of houses, flats, boarding houses and rooms, something which would set a pattern for the rest of her life. In Durbanville the family lived in their grandfather's house, remembered by Anna as 'the house with the pepper-tree'. The memoir of Fanie's son paints him as a high-spirited but also somewhat reckless man. His two granddaughters would remember him with great fondness, both referring to his exuberance as well as the jokes and laughter surrounding him despite his being bed-ridden with rheumatoid arthritis.[10] Information about this phase in Ingrid's life comes to us from a biographical sketch she wrote for *Die Vaderland*[11] and the first chapters of a memoir written by her sister Anna.[12] From these accounts it emerges that the years they spent in Durbanville were on the whole happy and free. Although not wealthy, they were part of a caring family; their mother and grandmother indulged them by taking part in their children's games and they could share in their grandfather's boisterous good humour. They roamed about freely in the rural atmosphere of Durbanville and the surrounding veld, where Ingrid was once attacked by a swarm of bees. They often visited relations in grand houses and on prosperous farms in the Paarl district. To the great consternation of their aunts, their mother allowed them to swim naked at family picnics – Ingrid once almost drowned in the Berg River. She was the more delicate of the two children, retaining a 'weak chest' after a bout of whooping cough.

It was also in Durbanville, Anna remembered, that Ingrid was christened at the age of three or four at an unconventional ceremony in the garden. Anna admitted to being jealous of Ingrid in her pretty little white dress and to watching the proceedings from a hiding-place in the neighbouring garden, an admission which also tells us something about the relationship between the sisters. The name Ingrid was frowned upon by the relations because it was not a family name, but her mother didn't pay any attention to their criticism. Their grandparents' attitude towards the church was unconventional for the time and community of which they were part. Grandfather Fanie was not a churchgoer and could even be suspected of religious indifference, his son conceded in his memoir, sometimes treating the dignified ministers of the Dutch Reformed Church with witty insouciance.[13] Grandmother Annie was a devout woman who later in life preferred to preach to coloured people or attend the Apostolic Church, because they were 'so lively and jolly', Ingrid later wrote.[14] Although she was never religious in the conventional sense of the word, Ingrid would retain the childlike and enduring faith in Jesus learnt from her grandmother for the rest of her life.

The Strand and Gordon's Bay
The death of their grandfather Fanie in 1938 brought an end to the relatively carefree life in Durbanville. With their grandfather gone, Ingrid and her sister Anna were now part of a household of women. In a sense they had two mothers: because of their mother's ill health, their grandmother Annie increasingly had to fulfil the role of mother and primary caretaker for the two girls. Their grandfather's death also left the small household financially destitute. They could not stay on in the house in Durbanville and had to move to the Strand in 1940. Their grandmother Annie's state pension was supplemented with small allowances from her sons A.C. and Jacob. Because of her health Beatrice could only work

intermittently; there was a short stint with the SABC in Cape Town as well as office jobs in Stellenbosch and the Strand. Their father also sent them money;[15] the divorce order stipulated that he should pay £5 per year towards the support of his children.[16] Although circumstances were difficult, Anna remembered that the two children were excited about their move to the Strand. They looked forward to living in a little house by the sea and being able to swim every day. To some extent their expectations were fulfilled. Even though they had to move from one house to another in the Strand and Gordon's Bay over the next few years, they both remembered the devotion with which their grandmother cared for them and their freedom to explore the sea, the veld and books. Although still young – Ingrid started kindergarten in July 1940 and Anna was put in Standard One in the Strand Primary School – their mother and grandmother allowed them greater freedom and mobility than was usual for the time. During their stay in Gordon's Bay they often wandered off into a pine forest on their way to school, to sit and read their books. Once they stayed away from school for so long that the teacher thought the family had moved again. Here, they were also allowed to keep small animals and continued exploring the veld and beach. They picked fruit from plants in the veld, gathered shellfish from the rock pools, played with tadpoles in the stream behind their house and buried small objects they called 'secrets' in the ground. It is not surprising that Gordon's Bay is one of the spaces that would later gain symbolic importance in Ingrid's poetry.

Their mother's illness cast a shadow over this relatively carefree time. During their first year in the Strand, Beatrice suffered a nervous breakdown and had to be hospitalised in Valkenburg psychiatric hospital in Cape Town. This traumatic experience greatly affected Ingrid and strengthened her bond with her grandmother, who was the only person to whom she could talk about it. In these circumstances their grandmother came to play an increasingly important role in their lives, caring for them as best she could within her limited means. Their meals often consisted of bread, soup or fish-heads and the children had to use a battered handbag of their grandmother's as a satchel for their schoolbooks. Grandmother Annie was the one who fostered Ingrid's talent as a writer by reading the poems Ingrid wrote from the age of six to the coloured congregations she preached to on Sundays.

Not long after her nervous breakdown Beatrice was diagnosed with cancer. When she was hospitalised in Somerset West her children tried to visit her as often as possible, either taking the bus or walking all the way from the Strand. Arriving at the hospital, they usually clambered on to her bed and were given food and cold drinks by the nurses. Despite the illness they were still able to share a bond of female confidentiality with their mother, telling her things about boyfriends and growing up that they could not mention to their devout grandmother. Ingrid would later write a short story, 'Eerste liefde' [First love], in which she expressed a young adolescent's desperate need to tell her uncomprehending grandmother about the first awakenings of love and desire. When Beatrice was later moved to Groote Schuur and then to the Conradie Hospital in Cape Town, they could not visit her as often. After spending almost two years in hospital, Beatrice died on 6 August 1944.[17] The bare facts of this narrative no doubt conceal great heartbreak and suffering for the grandmother and two children. Ingrid recalled her mother with great tenderness in the poem 'Ladybird':[18]

> Glans oker
> en 'n lig breek
> uit die see.
>
>> In die agterplaas
>> êrens tussen die wasgoed
>> en 'n boom vol granate
>> jou lag en die oggend
>> skielik en klein
>> soos 'n liewenheersbesie
>> geval op my hand
>
> [Gleaming ochre
> and a light breaks
> from the sea.
>
>> In the back yard

22

somewhere between the washing
and a pomegranate tree
your laugh and the morning
sudden and small
like a ladybird
fallen on my hand]

She wrote elsewhere: 'My moeder, sterwend, was so sonnig soos 'n liewenheersbesie, so vol geheime, so verrassend, so teer ...' [My mother, dying, was as sunny as a ladybird, so full of secrets, so surprising, so tender ...].[19]

Ingrid's early years, spent in the company of her mother and grandmother, had a profound influence on the rest of her life. Theirs was a home that gave the two girls tender and loving care but also exposed them to the suffering brought about by nervous disorder, illness and death. It was also an unconventional upbringing that allowed them to some degree the freedom to move outside the constraints of Afrikaner society of the day. Although their grandmother upheld strict religious values, their mother did not keep them on a tight rein. They could read what they liked, they were not as housebound as most children then and they treated people of other races with less of the prejudice and condescension usual at the time. They had little contact with their well-off relations, who seemed to lead more regulated and ordered lives. Their cousins in Stellenbosch lived in a house that was almost too neat and organised for them, while their rich aunt Joey Malan, who lived in Constantia, regarded them as 'wilde, ongetemde kinders' [wild, untamed children], according to Anna's unfinished memoir.

Beatrice's death brought an end to Ingrid's life within the intimacy of the maternal family. After the death of their mother in August, the two girls stayed on with their grandmother until their father Abraham came to fetch them in December 1944 and took them to live with him in Cape Town. The loss of two mothers within such a short space of time must have had an incalculable effect on the young Ingrid. A studio portrait, taken shortly before they left for Cape Town, shows Ouma Annie with her two granddaughters. Her face is wizened with age and her eyes deep-set; she is soberly attired in a black dress with a white crocheted collar. In contrast we see the freshness and youth of her two granddaughters. Dark-haired Anna on her right is 13 years old and on the brink of puberty; the blonde Ingrid on the other side is 11 and her wide smile is guileless, if somewhat posed. The photograph's pronounced contrast between youth and age emphasises rather than obscures the closeness between the old woman and the children. Surreptitiously Anna wrote their father a letter to say that they would prefer to stay with their grandmother and go to one of the local schools because they did not have clothes that were grand enough for Cape Town. But the letter had no effect and they had to leave their grandmother behind when Abraham fetched them. Although Ouma Annie died only in 1956 or 1957,[20] the

Ouma Annie with Anna and Ingrid Jonker. (Courtesy of the Ingrid Jonker Trust)

children rarely saw her after that painful farewell during which Ingrid tried to hold on to her grandmother's hand as long as possible.

Cape Town

In the years before their mother's death, the two children's contact with their father had been minimal. After his divorce from Beatrice there was a short-lived second marriage to one Barbara Gill before Abraham Jonker married Lulu Brewis, a writer of children's books, in 1941. Anna Jonker remembered that he once came to fetch her to spend a weekend with him while they were still living in Durbanville. Although he brought Ingrid a red top on that occasion, he did not acknowledge her presence at

25

all.[21] Because their father's house was not large enough to accommodate the two girls, Anna and Ingrid were put into lodgings in central Cape Town and attended a nearby school for the first six months of 1945.[22] They were fetched on Sundays to spend time with him and, after he bought a larger house in Plumstead, they went to live with him and his new family, wife Lulu and their two young children, Koos and Suzanne.

Anna and Ingrid each gave different accounts of their time in this house. According to Anna they were given a nice room with a balcony. She also remembered that though her father worked hard he made time for them when he could, reading them poetry and teaching Ingrid to waltz around the dining-room table.[23] Ingrid, on the other hand, later told Jack Cope and Laurens van der Post that they had to sit apart from the rest of the family at the dinner table and eat the food given to the servants.[24] Although it is difficult to gauge where the line between truth and fiction lies in these accounts, life with their stepmother Lulu was not easy for the two young girls. Although Lulu was kind to the girls when they were still boarding in Cape Town, things changed once they went to live with the family in Plumstead. In an interview, Anna once painted a dark picture of emotional deprivation and misunderstanding.[25] The two young girls' self-confidence was constantly undermined by snide remarks and there was little understanding for their physical needs as young girls entering puberty. André Brink remembered

26

that Ingrid recounted tales – with some exaggeration, he felt – in which Lulu lived up to the harsh stereotype of the fairytale stepmother.[26] Other friends also spoke of Ingrid's hostility towards her stepmother.[27] Although there was no love lost between the two girls and their stepmother, they had a good relationship with their much younger step-siblings, Koos and Suzanne. This is borne out by snapshots dating from this time which show the two sisters on the beach with Koos and Suzanne as well as other children. Although the photographs suggest that they were at least partly able to live out their love of the sea, the presence of rather severe-looking nannies in the pictures hints at a different life-style in Abraham and Lulu's house: more affluent, but also more structured, supervised and regulated. Outsiders observed that the relationship between Lulu and her stepdaughters was affected by the great difference between them. The children were used to wandering around on their own and expressing themselves freely; their stepmother wanted to exercise control and make them conform to strict middle-class values.[28] Their father seems to have been either powerless to intervene or too distracted by the demands of his career to take notice.

Who was this father who would influence Ingrid's life so profoundly? Abraham Jonker was a well-educated man who studied at the University of Stellenbosch from 1923 to 1930. Here he met the music student Beatrice Cilliers, whom he married in 1930. At Stellenbosch he obtained a bachelor's degree, majoring in Ancient Greek and Dutch, a master's degree in Ancient Greek and a diploma in theology (the last to please his parents rather than for his own sake). After two more years of studying law, he became an organiser for General Hertzog's National Party, before embarking on a career in journalism and working for publications like *Die Burger*, *Die Huisgenoot*, *Die Jongspan* and *Die Suiderstem*. He also had literary aspirations and published several novels and volumes of short stories, from the early 1930s onwards. The critical response to his literary work remained lukewarm, perhaps because his preference for the European-inspired 'Nuwe Saaklikheid' ('Modern Objectivity') was very different from the confessional mode newly popular in Afrikaans literature at the time. Because of the sombre worldview reflected in his writing, Ingrid Jonker's Dutch biographer Henk van Woerden typecast him as a secular Calvinist and described him as an aloof, panic-stricken puritan.[29] Although Abraham Jonker has been portrayed as the archetypal apartheid politician in the minds of those who know of the political tension that existed between him and his daughter, he had a chequered political career. In the election that brought D.F. Malan's National Party into power in 1948, he won a seat in parliament as a member of General Smuts's United Party. Together with other dissidents he formed the Conservative Party in 1954, but crossed the floor in 1956 to join the National Party.[30] Many of his contemporaries spoke of him as a political opportunist and turncoat.[31] Whether Abraham Jonker's changing political views were the result of careerism or inner conviction, they would later bring him into open confrontation with his daughter.

While living with their father and stepmother in Plumstead, Ingrid and her sister attended the English-medium Wynberg Girls' School. Ingrid was still in primary school when she started here in 1945, and she completed her matric in 1951. School reports indicate that she was a reasonably well-behaved girl ('Conduct: Fairly good and improved lately') and average student ('This is quite a creditable record'), who preferred to devote her energy to those subjects that really interested her. Writing seems to have been the one thing she cared about passionately. It was her teachers, rather than her literary-minded father, who recognised and encouraged her gift for writing.[32] Ingrid remembered that their headmistress, Miss Currie, reprimanded her for writing poems that satirised the schoolteachers, but was also the first person to declare that her young pupil had talent, even though she was undisciplined and disobedient.[33] Only a handful of Ingrid's schoolgirl poems survive.

Writing poems and stories seems to have been a way of creating a safe space for herself. In an article for *Drum* magazine in May 1963, Ingrid said of her childhood: 'I found a way of making my own happiness and I suppose that was the beginning of my poetry.' In a letter to André Brink she wrote: 'Miskien is digterwees maar 'n speelwêreld, nooit heeltemal die "diepe erns" nie, maar vir my safe soos Jesus' [Maybe being a poet is a play world, never completely serious, but for me safe as Jesus].[34] Apart from creating a place to which she could retreat and in which she could feel at home, writing also helped her gain self-confidence. Sending her poems to magazines and being paid for them was a means of achieving some independence and a sense of self-worth. An autobiographical short story "n Daad van geloof' [An act of faith], written shortly before her death, confirms this. It tells how a little girl decides to sell her poems to buy herself a satchel and so help ease the burden on her grandmother who had to care for her. Several poems and stories appeared in the children's magazine *Die Jongspan* in 1947 when she was 14.[35]

It seems that Ingrid was set on a literary career from early on. In 1949, when she was only 16, she submitted a volume of poems to Nasionale Boekhandel titled *Na die somer* [After the summer]. It was not accepted but she was invited by the publisher's reader, D.J. Opperman, to discuss her poems with him. As Opperman was one of the foremost Afrikaans poets of the day and a hugely influential figure in the Afrikaans literary world, Ingrid was nervous about meeting him but was encouraged by the fact that he took her seriously and gave her good advice.[36] On two occasions in 1951 she again sent him poems on which he commented, inviting her to send more. Some of these poems (for instance 'Skrik' and

'Keuse') include veiled hints at romantic longing and an awakening sexuality, often reined in by feelings of religious guilt. It is difficult to reconstruct the inner life of the adolescent Ingrid on the basis of these poems, because the expression of feeling in them is still guarded, hemmed in by schoolgirl decorum and the writerly rhetoric of a previous generation of Afrikaans poets.

After passing matric in 1951 it was clear Ingrid wanted to leave home. Anna remembered that she came from Johannesburg, where she was working at the time, to help Ingrid negotiate with their father about her leaving. After the children told him that there was 'space in the house but no place in the heart' for them, he agreed that Ingrid could move out. Anna then helped her set herself up in a boarding house in the centre of Cape Town.[37] In this way Ingrid left behind yet another of the many homes she would occupy during the course of her life.

3

Early adulthood, marriage and motherhood, 1952–1958

'It was still the time of believing in yourself and your own creativity and how you were going to change the whole world before you're thirty and committing suicide afterwards, dying happily ever after'.

– *Nico Hagen in* Ingrid Jonker: Her lives and time

Office-worker

That Ingrid did not get the opportunity to attend university is a recurrent theme in many of her friends' recollections of her. Most of them blamed her father for depriving her of the opportunity. Others attributed it to the influence of Ingrid's stepmother Lulu.[38] Abraham Jonker did support Ingrid financially while she attended a secretarial course in Cape Town in 1952, the year after she matriculated. This enabled her to become financially independent and support herself. She held a series of jobs as secretary, proofreader, translator and bookshop assistant in the years that followed, working for firms like the publisher Kennis, Citadel Press, HAUM Publishers, Culemborg Publishers, Nasionale Boekhandel and the Cape Divisional Council. She also helped Louis Hiemstra while he was revising the *Tweetalige woordeboek* [Bilingual Dictionary].[39] Her employers' impressions of her varied. While she was highly commended by Hiemstra as a proofreader, Cor Pama found her a muddle-headed and ineffective bookshop assistant. Many people remembered her dedication as a proofreader, but she often felt frustrated and unfulfilled in the jobs she held.

Although she had to become a working woman to provide for herself, Ingrid remained dedicated to the vocation of poet which she had set for herself as a schoolgirl. 'I became an office worker, but the real thing I lived for was to write,' she professed in the article for *Drum.* She continued sending her poems for publication in a variety of popular magazines like *Die Huisgenoot, Naweekpos* and *Rooi Rose*[40] as well as the literary journal *Standpunte.* It was clear that her poems were gradually becoming more sophisticated and accomplished. During this time Ingrid also pursued other artistic interests. She took lessons with the Spanish sculptor Florencio Cuairan, and attended classes in elocution and drama. It comes as no surprise that, when one listens to tape recordings of her reading her own poetry, what impresses one is the clarity of her diction and articulation. Her voice is that of a cultured woman, calm and confident. Although she gave the impression of being vulnerable and defenceless, there must also have been a measure of resilience and determination in her character to have enabled her to overcome the deprivation of her early years and develop artistically and socially after she left her father's house. Jack Cope would voice the same sentiment in a letter he wrote to Uys Krige in May 1959, when he said that her friends did not always 'make allowances for her basic strength and perseverance'.[41] There are other contradictions in the photographs dating from this time. Some of them portray her as a pert office-worker with a high-collared dress or neat blouse behind a typewriter. Other snapshots show her as a young *bohemienne* in shorts with tanned legs and a cigarette between her fingers. In an interview conducted a few years later she admitted to smoking 30 cigarettes a day, adding that she did not eat much because she thought food was boring.[42]

There is a tendency to define Ingrid in terms of her relationships with men and to forget her friendships and relationships with women. During these first years of her adult life she built up a wide circle of both male and female friends. Her male friends included the actor Jannie Gildenhuys and Ernst Eloff, who are shown in photographs with her. She shared a number of flats with woman friends with whom she kept up a correspondence in later years. Lena Oelofse was one of her first flatmates, and later Jean (Bambi) du Preez. Several other names would crop up in the years that followed: Bonnie Davidtsz, Marie Swart, Marie Prinsloo, Margo Holt,

Hélène Roos and Elmie Watson. There were also close, possibly intimate, friendships with the writers Berta Smit (her supervisor at Citadel Press to whom she showed and read her poems) and Freda Linde (who worked for the publishers HAUM and John Malherbe). Ingrid formed strong bonds as well with older women like the artist Marjorie Wallace, who became something of a mother figure for her, and the encyclopaedist Juliana Bouws, whose friendship provided her with invaluable emotional support. In 1954, three years after she left school, she met her future husband Piet Venter at a party in Sea Point.

First volume, *Ontvlugting*

The publication of Ingrid's first volume of poems, *Ontvlugting* [Escape], in June 1956 was the culmination of her desire to be a published poet. Although her debut volume attracted the attention of the important critics of the time, their reviews mostly emphasised its adolescent youthfulness and thematic 'slimness'. While *Ontvlugting* may be limited in its formal and thematic scope, it was clearly the product of a self-conscious poet who took her work seriously. It suggested that Ingrid Jonker was not just an intuitive poet whose poems came effortlessly, but someone who carefully crafted and revised her work. Although the volume is technically still somewhat awkward because of its over-use of rhyming couplets, most of the poems demonstrate sensitivity for the texture and musicality of words as well as their semantic potential. Uys Krige would later refer to her 'skulpfyn oor' (ear as finely tuned as a sea-shell).

The title poem sets the tone for the rest of the volume as well as for the Ingrid Jonker oeuvre, introducing the contexts, themes and images that would occur again and again in her work. Following after the Afrikaans is a translation by André Brink and Antjie Krog.

Ontvlugting

Uit hierdie Valkenburg het ek ontvlug
en dink my nou in Gordonsbaai terug:

Ek speel met paddavisse in 'n stroom
en kerf swastikas in 'n rooikransboom

Ek is die hond wat op die strande draf
en dom-allenig teen die aandwind blaf

Ek is die seevoël wat verhongerd daal
en dooie nagte opdis as 'n maal

Die god wat jou geskep het uit die wind
sodat my smart in jou volmaaktheid vind:

My lyk lê uitgespoel in wier en gras
op al die plekke waar ons eenmaal was.

Escape

From this Valkenburg have I run away
and in my thoughts return to Gordon's Bay:

I play with tadpoles swimming free
carve swastikas in a red-krantz tree

I am the dog that slinks from beach to beach
barks dumb-alone against the evening breeze

I am the gull that swoops in famished flights
to serve up meals of long-dead nights

The god who shaped you from the wind and dew
to find fulfilment of my pain in you:

Washed out my body lies in weed and grass
in all the places where we once did pass.

Although one must remember that poems are fictional constructs, the two spaces mentioned in the first lines of this poem have a particular resonance in Ingrid Jonker's life. Valkenburg is the psychiatric hospital to which her mother was committed after a breakdown; Gordon's Bay is the seaside town where she spent part of her youth with her mother, grandmother and sister. The speaker begins by referring to the fact that she is confined in 'this Valkenburg' and that she escapes from this space associated with mental illness by returning to her memories of Gordon's Bay. Although biographical information suggests that Ingrid remembered Gordon's Bay as a place where she felt happy and secure despite her family's poverty, the poem implies that this space already contains the germ of future unhappiness, isolation and death. When the speaker thinks herself back in Gordon's Bay, the images of herself that come up are those of someone carving swastikas in a tree-trunk, a lonely dog on the beach, a hungry seagull and a god who creates in order to 'fulfil' pain. The poem's final lines present yet another image that confirms the sombre content of the childhood paradise, that of the speaker's corpse washed up on the beach in all the places she had visited in the past. These lines are among the best-known and most resonant in Afrikaans literature, because of the eerie precision with which they predicted Ingrid Jonker's suicide by drowning. Many have said that they constituted a prophecy which she could not escape fulfilling. In his review of the volume, Rob Antonissen wrote that he found much of the volume 'facile', but that the poems also had a 'curt matter-of-factness' which provokes the reader. This is certainly true of the poem 'Ontvlugting', which presents us with the first of a series of disturbing images of the self in the volume, that of the lonely dog, the hungry gull, the capricious creator, the washed-up corpse.

Even at this early stage many of the poems in the volume reflect on love's disillusions rather than its joys, love's failure rather than its fulfilment. They ponder resignation, dependence, the duplicitous mirror-play of reality and illusion, sorrow, farewell and the loss of innocence. An interesting feature of some of the poems is the way in which different male figures are folded into one, that of the lover, the father and God or Christ, as in the poems 'Offerande' [Sacrifice] and 'Jy het vir my gesterf' [You have died for me]. The volume also gives an indication of the poet's ability to imagine herself, chameleon-like, in the bodies of others and to take on different voices. A few poems contain the germ of rebellion against the bourgeois values of society as well as a sensitivity to the injustices of the political situation in South Africa, especially 'Die blommeverkoopster' [The flower-seller], written from the perspective of a coloured woman in love with a white man.

While the poet is able to imagine herself in the bodies and situations of others in this volume, her poetry also reveals an indisputably female consciousness. It is important to note that Ingrid Jonker's small body of poetry, starting with the volume *Ontvlugting*, infused the largely male domain of Afrikaans poetry with a female thematic and lexicon. The only other strong female poets active in the Afrikaans literary tradition by the time Ingrid Jonker made her debut were Elisabeth Eybers, Olga Kirsch, Ina Rousseau and Sheila Cussons. In the poem 'Ontnugtering' [Disillusionment], written after a visit to Johannesburg in 1955, the speaker refers to the fact that she wanted to deceive the world by presenting herself as a doll (a toy as well as a feminine or sexual object). But the truth has come out: she is a 'verwronge digter' [misshapen poet] who knows she will be mocked by the world but defiantly invites it to do so. The poem reflects an awareness of the creative woman's tenuous position in society: the doll-like woman is acceptable, the misshapen poetess is not. The journalist Dot van der Merwe's article about the publication of *Ontvlugting* in *Die Burger* on 23 June 1956 proved the point by referring to Ingrid as the daughter of the MP Abraham Jonker and mentioning the fact that her fiancé Piet Venter found some of the poems in the volume too revealing.

This same article put into circulation the story of Abraham Jonker's ungenerous reaction when presented with the volume. He was reported to have said that he hoped there was something between the covers of the book and that he would look at it later, fully expecting her to have shamed him with its content.[43] Whether he really made this remark or not, it is true that the relationship between literary fathers and their literary daughters is always a potentially fraught one. There certainly seems to have been room for complex reciprocal feelings of admiration and envy in this case. Abraham Jonker was a published writer, even though he achieved only a modest reputation in the Afrikaans literary canon. According to friends, Ingrid was in awe of her father (she referred to him as a 'writer of note' in an early autobiographical piece) and desperately wanted him to acknowledge her work. On the other hand, it is possible that he felt threatened by the talent of his rebellious daughter. This may have been the reason why he treated her in the off-hand, casual way which dismayed her friends. Berta Smit observed that Ingrid was always a little self-conscious and unsure of herself in his presence, as if she felt inferior towards him.[44] Their relationship became more and more complex as their political views started to differ.

A new circle of friends and the university on the beach
Publication of her first volume of poetry provided Ingrid with entry into an exciting, new world. This happened as the result of her introduction to the writer Jan Rabie, who worked for the SABC and conducted an interview with her for radio in 1956. She soon became close friends with Jan and his wife, the painter Marjorie Wallace, who shared a house in Green Point with the painters Erik Laubscher and his wife Claude Bouscharain. Ingrid would later develop a crush on Jan, which was not reciprocated. He referred to her as Ingrid Muisvoet [Ingrid Mousefoot] because of her light little footsteps and the chaos she left in her wake.[45] Ingrid was taken up in the Rabies' large circle of friends, which included Uys Krige, Jack Cope, Adam Small, Richard Rive, Peter Clarke, Breyten Breytenbach, James Matthews, Kenny Parker, Piet Philander, Gillian Jewell, Harry Bloom and Albie Sachs.[46] Meeting these people broadened her literary horizons by exposing her to the work of a range of writers she had not known before. She began to read the work of Spanish, Dutch, American, French and Italian poets and came to know the writing of Federico Garcia Lorca, Pablo Neruda, Paul Éluard, Sybren Polet, Gerrit Achterberg, Lucebert, Dylan Thomas and e.e. cummings (one of whose poems she

41

Ingrid Jonker and Jan Rabie on Clifton beach. (Courtesy of the National English Literary Museum, Grahamstown)

later translated into Afrikaans). Some of these writers she came to know through Uys Krige's translations of poems in Spanish, French and Italian.

Among the group of friends, she felt a special affinity for Uys Krige, who soon became her mentor. He read her poems with a sharply critical eye, advising her to revise her work constantly. Krige was so stern a reader that she referred to him as 'the Iceman',[47] a play on the name Uys and Eugene O'Neill's play *The iceman cometh.* He was the one who encouraged her the most, even though he would tick her off about certain lines and sometimes laugh at her, she later said in a radio interview about her career as a poet.[48] It was Krige who introduced her to the work of surrealist poets like Éluard, whose work he translated into Afrikaans, leading her to experiment with free verse and abandon the formal rigidity of her first volume.

Ingrid's introduction to this 'bohemian' circle of friends also proved to be a political education. Through her contact with Jan Rabie and his friends, she became part of a social circle that was indifferent to the colour bar imposed by apartheid politics. Many of her new friends were 'coloured' in the racial taxonomy of the day: Richard Rive, Kenny Parker, Peter Clarke, Adam Small and Piet Philander. Although she was to a large extent free of racial prejudice (or 'racial feelings', as she later phrased it in the *Drum* article) because of the unconventional way in which she spent her early childhood, she told Peter Clarke that social interaction with people of other races was something new for her.[49] She became close friends with Richard Rive, whom she often visited; he remembers in his autobiography *Writing black* that they drove around Cape Town on a scooter, pretending to be brother and

43

sister because Marjorie Wallace said they looked alike and she felt motherly towards both of them.[50]

Another meeting place during these years was the Clifton bungalow 'Sea Girt' which Uys Krige shared with the writer Jack Cope from September 1958 until 1968.[51] Uys and Jack had known each other since the late 1940s and bought this house together after Jack's wife Lesley left him and moved to White River in April 1958 with their sons Raymond and Michael.[52] Jack and Uys even had the dubious honour of becoming known as the 'Clifton Mafia',[53] for having to write letters of refusal to aspiring writers in their capacity as editors of the literary journal *Contrast*, set up by Jack and others in 1960.[54] Ingrid met Jack in August 1957 when he returned the key of Ingrid and her husband Piet's flat on behalf of Uys Krige, who had stayed there for a while.[55] Many people's memories of Ingrid are framed by Clifton and several photographs show her on Clifton beach, first with Piet, later with Marjorie, Jan, Uys, Jack and other friends. Marjorie remembered her as always laughing, tanned, barefoot, in and out of the sea, kicking a ball on the beach with Jan, Jack and Uys.[56]

Although the properties above Clifton's beaches are today home to the extremely wealthy, the area was originally laid out by the City of Cape Town for demobilised soldiers who had fought in the First World War. In order to help overcome a serious housing shortage, they were allowed to erect bungalows on small plots in Clifton, some of them built out of the packing cases used for

44

importing cars in the 1920s and 1930s. Michael Cope, son of Jack, writes in his autobiographical work *Intricacy* that the people who lived there in the 1950s and 1960s were from the 'middle-class or lower middle-class, bohemians and the like'.[57] He also quotes Albie Sachs, who recalled that Clifton's were the only beaches in Cape Town that did not display racial segregation signs and also spoke of New Year's Eve parties there that seemed like a 'truce from apartheid for twenty-four hours', with people of all races attending.[58] Sachs remembered as well the electrifying effect that a lecture by Uys Krige on the work and life of the Spanish poet Lorca had on him: 'What Uys did, he connected the intimacy and soulfulness and inwardness of the poetry, which was a very intense internal dialogue with yourself and your emotional vocabulary and your literary vocabulary with the grand public events of the world ... So, I didn't discover culture while I was in politics, it was culture that actually took me into politics.'[59] Sachs's anecdote gives an idea of the impassioned intellectual sphere into which Ingrid was drawn through her contact with Jan, Uys and later also Jack. It was an intellectual world in which not only literary matters were discussed but also the politics of the day, even though their actual involvement in political life was limited. It was later said that Ingrid's university was Sea Girt and that the Clifton bohemians held their salon on the beach, the place where they read their poetry.[60] Ingrid herself would later refer to the 'good old Clifton literary rush' in a letter to a friend.[61]

45

A young Ingrid Jonker. (Courtesy of the National English Literary Museum)

Breyten Breytenbach, who was part of the circle of friends before he left for Europe in 1960, later used the term 'moral schizophrenia' to describe life on Clifton beach in the 1950s: 'We were lying on Clifton beach while we knew what was happening on the other side of the mountain, on the Cape flats,' he said.[62] Ingrid's contact with Cape Town's liberal-minded set led to further tension with her father, who later blamed them for many of her problems.

Marriage and motherhood

As well as developing as a poet and politically conscious individual, Ingrid also became a married woman and mother. As for many women writers of her time, it would prove difficult for her to reconcile her roles as poet, wife and mother. Her husband-to-be, Piet Venter, was himself an aspiring writer and poet. At that stage he worked for a company that took tourists on safari through Africa. He was 15 years older than Ingrid, leading many people to speculate that a father complex lay at the root of her attraction to him. The two got married in a ceremony in the Congregational Church in Paarl on 15 December 1956, with Ingrid's father giving her away. The wedding photographs, taken by Tom Burgers but never collected by the couple, show Ingrid in a knee-length white dress and wide-brimmed hat, with a brittle smile and bright eyes. Her friend Berta Smit, who played the organ at the wedding, was relieved that Ingrid had abandoned her plans to get married in bare feet and a Greek toga or kaftan on Paarl Mountain, but felt that the whole ceremony was a tense and uncomfortable affair.[63] Many of her friends tried to dissuade her from marrying the older Venter, but apparently she was determined to get married and have a child. Venter's second wife Topsi recalled that although he was very much in love with Ingrid, he was actually hesitant to marry her. And when he wanted to back out of the marriage, she tried to commit suicide.[64] The threat of suicide is another of the leitmotifs that emerge when friends and family recount their memories of Ingrid. Exactly when it became a serious problem is difficult to reconstruct.

Ingrid and Piet's daughter Simone was born almost a year later, on 1 December 1957. The letters written during this time all speak of her excitement about the coming event. At the same time she was inspired by her pregnancy to write the powerful but disturbing poem 'Swanger vrou' [Pregnant woman]. Although it was only published in her second volume, *Rook en oker* [Smoke and ochre], in 1963, the manuscript is dated 1957. The Afrikaans is followed by André Brink and Antjie Krog's translation:

Swanger vrou

Ek lê onder die kors van die nag singend,
opgekrul in die riool, singend,
en my nageslag lê in die water.

Ek speel ek is kind:
appelliefies, appelliefies en heide,
koekmakrankas, anys,
en die paddavis gly
in die slym in die stroom,
in my liggaam
my skuimwit gestalte;
maar riool o riool
my nageslag lê in die water.

Nóg singend vliesrooi ons bloedlied,
ek en my gister,
my gister hang onder my hart,
my kalkoentjie, my wiegende wêreld,
en my hart wat sing soos 'n besie
my besie-hart sing soos 'n besie;
maar riool o riool,
my nageslag lê in die water.

Ek speel ek is bly:
kyk wáár spat die vuurvlieg!
die maanskyf, 'n nat snoet wat beef –
maar met die môre, die hinkende vroedvrou
koulik en grys op die skuiwende heuwels
stoot ek jou uit deur die kors in die daglig,
o treurende uil, groot uil van die daglig,
los van my skoot maar besmeer
met my trane besmeer
en besmet met verdriet.

Riool o riool
ek lê bewend singend,
hoe anders as bewend
met my nageslag onder jou water …?

Pregnant woman

Under the crust of the night I lie singing,
curled up in the sewer, singing,
and my offspring lies in the water.

I play I'm a child:
gooseberries, gooseberries and heather,
kukumakrankas, aniseed,
and the tadpole slides
in the slime in the stream,
in my body
my foamwhite figure;
but sewer o sewer,
my offspring lies in the water.

Membrane red of bloodsong still singing,
I and my yesterday,
my yesterday suspended under my heart,
my kalkoentjie, my swaying world,
and my heart that sings like a cicada
my cicada heart sings like a cicada;
but sewer o sewer
my offspring lies in the water.

I play I'm happy:
look how far the firefly splashes!
the moonslice, a wet snout that quivers –
but with the morning, the limping midwife
chilly and grey on the shifting hills,
I push you out through the crust into daylight,

o grieving owl, great owl of daylight,
freed from my womb but soiled
soiled with my tears
and infected with sadness.

Sewer o sewer,
I lie shivering singing,
how else but shivering
with my offspring submerged in your water ...?

The first stanza evokes the potent image of a pregnant woman, who lies curled up in a sewer while she is singing what may be the poem we are reading. Although the line 'my offspring lies in the water' suggests that the baby is still safely ensconced in the waters of the womb, there are also veiled hints of miscarriage or abortion. Even though the stanzas that follow try to evoke positive images of childlike playfulness during the conception of the child (stanza 2), of a singing body that tenderly cradles the unborn child (stanza 3) and of playing at being happy (stanza 4), the refrains of these stanzas keep returning to the ambiguous image of the unborn child lying in the water. Ultimately the birth of the child is seen as something sorrowful: it is pushed out of the womb, 'soiled' with tears and 'infected with sadness' (stanza 4). The poem's conclusion returns to the image of the first stanza, with the speaker now not only singing, but also shivering, while her offspring lies submerged in the waters of the sewer ('submerged in *your* water'). The baby is no longer safely enveloped in the waters of the womb, but has been pushed out of the womb into the sewer of life to be with its mother. The birth of the child elicits fear rather than joy. The final lines suggest that both mother and child are the result of 'mis-births' that have deposited them in a sewer rather than a happy and productive life. Even though this poem gives the impression of a spontaneous cry of distress, it is clear from Ingrid's correspondence with Uys Krige that she carefully worked and reworked this poem. It was also starkly different from the poems about motherhood written by Ingrid's precursors in the Afrikaans female literary tradition. Indeed it is closer in tone to the poems on motherhood and childbirth that the American poet Sylvia Plath would write a few years later in the early 1960s, and it came to exert a strong influence on future poets in Afrikaans like Antjie Krog and Marlise Joubert.

Despite this rather ominous poem, the birth of daughter Simone on 1 December 1957 was the realisation of a dream for Ingrid and a high point in her life. The photographs of her and baby Simone reflect the pride and absorption of any young mother in her baby. Because Piet and Ingrid lived in successive flats in Sea Point and Clifton, baby Simone became part of Ingrid's life in her new circle of friends and is often pictured among them on the beach.

Although many of Ingrid's friends made their living from their art, she kept up her office jobs during her pregnancy and after the birth of her daughter. In April 1957 she wrote to Uys Krige that she would remain with Aat Kaptein's publishing house Culemborg until the end of June before quitting to wait for the birth of her baby. In the year after Simone's birth she again worked for the publisher HAUM. She also earned extra money by modelling for the magazine *Sjarme* [Charm], whose editor, Hélène Roos, was a friend of hers. Hélène commented that Ingrid was a natural model because she had the ability to be different people for different occasions. The pictures, which show Ingrid modelling a bra and petticoat, a bikini and pyjamas on Clifton beach, confirm her ability to act out the roles required of her.

It was from this life that Piet Venter took her when his company transferred him to Johannesburg. His relationship with her new circle of friends had proved to be problematic from the outset. Although he and Uys were friends, it is clear from the interviews given in later years by people like Marjorie Wallace that they regarded him as vain and found him intellectually inferior. Ingrid's close friendship with Jan, and also Jack, during this time verged on the intimate, even though it did not develop into anything serious. Jack's 1958 diary shows that she spent a lot of time in the company of these men, as well as with Uys, and that she sometimes even talked of her 'romance' with the unyielding Jan. Piet eventually became resentful of his young wife's easy-going life-style while he had to provide for the family, and decided to take a job in

Johannesburg. At the beginning of May 1959 the couple moved to Johannesburg when their daughter Simone was 17 months old.

4

Separation, divorce and a new relationship, 1959–1962

> 'I thought of what the child might have been had
> he been allowed to live. I thought what could be
> reached, what could be gained by death?'
> — *Ingrid Jonker in* Drum, *May 1963*

Johannesburg

Ingrid's move to Johannesburg proved to be a rude awakening to the realities of life in South Africa for which the bohemian idyll of Clifton had not prepared her. The letters that she wrote to the friends left behind in Cape Town give an indication of how she experienced life in Johannesburg on arriving there. The family lived in a kind of boarding house, the Rondawels, in Illovo before moving to a rented house in Emmarentia. Ingrid desperately missed her friends and the sea; she found Johannesburg boring, primitive, materialistic and ugly. She felt cooped up and resented the weekend drives through the Johannesburg suburbs to look for a house where they could settle. Only when the couple moved to a flat in Hillbrow in December 1959 did she feel more at home in the city: 'This slum suits my heart better than Emmarentia, one sees the life here although only from the balcony,' she wrote to Jack Cope.[65]

On first arriving in Johannesburg, she was appalled by the attitudes of many of the people she met. Shortly after their arrival she wrote to Jack that the other boarders talked of 'Kaffirs' and 'Wogs' and that Simone was called 'Simone Afrikaander' by their children; at the same time her fellow Afrikaners looked down on her because she was a poet and regarded her as an 'artistic type' who was not one of them. The name of Prime Minister Hendrik Verwoerd cropped up more than once in her correspondence. In a letter dated 1 June 1959 she told Jan about a speech that Verwoerd made at a language festival in Pretoria, referring to him as 'die verleier van ons volk' [the seducer of our volk] who had basked in the applause of white Afrikanerdom after his speech. She was bitter about the fact that the poetry of the younger generation and that of coloured poets were largely ignored and that coloured people were not allowed to attend the festival. She also said that she was being denounced as a liberal and told of an incident in which her husband's brother-in-law François Smuts forbade her to set foot in his house again after a political argument in which she announced she had coloured friends. In a pun on Verwoerd's name she wrote that Smuts was like a 'Verwoerde dier' (a 'verwoede dier' being an 'enraged animal').

After only three months in Johannesburg, Ingrid fled and returned to Cape Town, leaving both her husband and child behind. It was her unhappiness in Johannesburg and the increasing dissatisfaction with her marriage that led to her hurried departure. Things had reached breaking point when Piet suspected her of a flirtation with their lodger, the actor Pietro Nolte. Because he was so violently upset, Ingrid agreed to leave Simone behind when she departed for Cape Town. Breyten Breytenbach, who was also staying with the family while on tour through South Africa, wrote to tell Jan Rabie that Ingrid was in love with him and on her way to Cape Town to be with him. Back in Cape Town, Ingrid first stayed with Jan and Marjorie, then with her father in St James (he insisted that she stay married) before getting a flat in Clifton. It was not long before Ingrid was back in Johannesburg. Piet travelled to Cape Town with Simone to persuade Ingrid to come back. After he had a fainting fit at a party while Ingrid was dancing with Jack, she agreed to return to Johannesburg with him. Her despair at being back in the marriage surfaced in dark comments about a death wish. Five days after she arrived back in Johannesburg she wrote to Jack: 'I still want to die.' A month later she told him in a letter: 'I would be glad if you do not take my death-wish in a literature [*sic*] way.'[66] To Uys she wrote that the whole experience was a waking nightmare and much more complicated than anyone could understand. Piet Venter's version of events, albeit in a fictionalised form, was given in fragments of an unpublished novel, *Biografie van 'n onbekende* [Biography of a stranger].

Even though Ingrid was desperately unhappy in Johannesburg she did not stop writing and reading. From letters to friends it emerges that she was writing poetry and was considering the possibility of publishing a second volume. But she was uncertain whether she should submit another volume for publication without the help of Uys Krige, who was then away on an extended trip in the USA and Europe.[67] She regularly reported on her reading in letters to friends, discussing her likes and dislikes with them. She felt a great affinity for the Welsh poet Dylan Thomas, to whom she dedicated the poem '25 December 1959', and was also reading the work of contemporary Dutch poets and plays by Eugene O'Neill. It was during this time that she wrote a letter to *Die Burger*, criticising the established poet and critic W.E.G. Louw for his insensitive review of a performance of a play by the Belgian writer Hugo Claus, *'n Bruid in die môre* [A bride in the morning]. She defended the play's criticism of a materialist society for its cynical and immoral attitude towards the idealism of the youth. That it took considerable courage to oppose an established critic in this way is shown by her speculation about the possible consequences in a letter to Jack: 'Do you think WEG Louw will have his knife in for me when my book appears? Needless question. I'm so afraid of people that I get the shivers when I've been with them every time, yet I must always do things of which I'm afraid.'[68] This comment gives us yet another perspective on Ingrid's personality: scared but determined as well to speak her mind, afraid but also fearless. This characteristic may have been part of the strange logic of her suicide a few years later.

It was probably her interest in the theatre and her contact with theatre people like Bartho Smit, Kita Redelinghuys, Pietro Nolte, Richard Daneel and Lydia Lindeque (Uys Krige's ex-wife) that inspired Ingrid during this time to write what would be her only play, *'n Seun na my hart* [A son after my own heart].[69] Although only a short one-act play, it is rich in psychological resonance. The main character is an elderly woman, Anna, who lives in reduced circumstances and worships her Aryan-looking son who was killed in the war. Her lyrical reminiscences are taken up by her friend Maria, who is a spinster and has an almost erotic longing for a son of her own. The third character in the play is the son himself, who, it turns out, has not died in the war and is a degenerate version of the son that Anna imagines she had. He is a swarthy cripple, he drinks and visits prostitutes. Certain ideas about contemporary society (possibly inspired by Ingrid's stay in Johannesburg) are developed around the figure of this son. From his perspective as an impoverished man on crutches rejected by his mother, he casts an acerbic look at society. His railing against the privileged and their empty pronouncements comes to a climax in the following words (my translation of the Afrikaans): 'Justice, they say, dignity, truth, values! Social workers, missionaries, charity! *My* wife! *My* husband! *My* children! *My* parents! *My* family! *My* friends! *My* country! *My* language! *My* church! What I believe, they say, and I don't understand it. Humaneness and I don't know what they are talking about. Morality, and it means nothing to me. Apartheid, they say, and I spit on it. Solitude, they say, and I piss on it.'

He wants to change the outdated ways of doing and seeing of the people around him, but to be able to do so he needs his mother to accept him as he is, her sick and disabled child. The play's conclusion shows that this will not happen: his mother continues to talk past him about her imaginary dead child, while Maria sustains her self-deception by translating her real son's words into concepts that Anna can accommodate. Although the play seems to revolve around the personal relationship between mother and child, it also has political overtones. The rebellious son wants moral and political renewal, whereas his mother lives in the past and glorifies the memory of an imaginary son who lived out the ideals of another kind of life, that of farm-boy and soldier. The play hints at its author's own futile attempts to communicate her ideals to her father and also gives expression to 'die leuen van ons land' [the lie of our country], to quote the actress Joey de Koker.[70] Ironically, an attempt to perform the play (as well as a reading of Ingrid's poems) in Swellendam two years after her death was cancelled because of a complaint by three Dutch Reformed ministers that the event would promote the work of the Sestigers. It was eventually performed for the first time in 1970 in the Johannesburg Civic Theatre.

By the end of January 1960, not long after the move to Hillbrow, Ingrid finally left her husband after a marriage of three years and returned to Cape Town with their daughter Simone. The divorce papers filed by Ingrid's lawyer referred to difficulties in the marriage and indicated that Piet requested her to leave.[71] Their divorce would only be finalised two years later, on 30 January 1962. It seems that Piet and Ingrid remained on relatively good terms after their separation and divorce, with both trying to minimise its effects on Simone. As Ingrid did not receive adequate maintenance to support her child, she was obliged to take a job and put Simone in a nursery school. Piet would also make periodic threats that he would try to gain sole custody of Simone; these greatly unnerved Ingrid. Once more, the jobs she took were related to the book industry and publishing: she worked in the publicity section of Nasionale Boekhandel in Elsies River in 1960,[72] for Nasionale Pers in 1961 and later as an assistant in a bookshop. She also did freelance typing for Uys Krige as well as proofreading and translation for F.L. Alexander, the arts critic for *Die Burger*. Back in Cape Town, Ingrid and Simone first stayed in her father's house in St James before moving to a flat in Bantry Bay and then to the cottage 'Deining' above Clifton's Moses Beach, which they shared with her friend Margo Holt.[73]

Writing 'Die kind'

A few months after arriving back in Cape Town, Ingrid wrote the poem 'Die kind' in response to political events of the time. In March 1960 the PAC, under the leadership of Robert Sobukwe, pre-empted the ANC's plans to launch a campaign against the pass laws on 31 March. Sobukwe called on black people to leave their pass books at home and to present themselves, non-violently, for arrest at police stations on 21 March. In Sharpeville near Johannesburg police eventually opened fire when a crowd of approximately 10,000 people turned up at the police station, killing 69 people and injuring more than 180. Later on the same day police also clashed with protesters at Langa, a township in Cape Town, shooting three people and injuring several others.

The incident that gave rise to the writing of 'Die kind' occurred in Nyanga township on 1 April when a car on its way to take a sick child to hospital was stopped by members of the South African Defence Force at a road-block and ordered to turn around. As one of the passengers in the car later recalled, the driver told the soldiers that his car could not reverse and proceeded to make a U-turn. As the car started to move they opened fire, presumably because they thought the driver wanted to force his way through. The windows of the car were shattered and a 20-month-old boy, Wilberforce Mazuli Manjati, was hit by one of the bullets. After the shooting the child was rushed to Groote Schuur Hospital but he was already dead on arrival, his great-aunt Edna Mombuyiselo Manjati recalled more than 45 years later in an interview with a reporter.[74] The child's body was then taken to the police station at Philippi.

Ingrid wrote the poem in a rush of anger and indignation after she heard of the incident,[75] and also visited the scene.[76] When she tried to have it published a few months later in June, first in the National Party-aligned newspaper *Die Burger* and then in the United Party newspaper *Weekblad*, the editors of both indignantly turned her down. The poem was eventually published in *Contrast* in July 1961 and immediately attracted attention. It was reprinted in the Netherlands, broadcast in English by the BBC, translated into a variety of languages and also published in Hindi in India.[77] The publication of English and Zulu translations of the poem in *Drum* magazine in May 1963 made it known among a wider South African audience. What follows is the Afrikaans version of the poem and its translation into English by Jack Cope and William Plomer.[78]

Die kind wat doodgeskiet is deur soldate by Nyanga
Die kind is nie dood nie
die kind lig sy vuiste teen sy moeder
wat Afrika skreeu   skreeu die geur

van vryheid en heide
in die lokasies van die omsingelde hart

Die kind lig sy vuiste teen sy vader
in die optog van die generasies
wat Afrika skreeu   skreeu die geur
van geregtigheid en bloed
in die strate van sy gewapende trots

Die kind is nie dood nie
nóg by Langa nóg by Nyanga
nóg by Orlando nóg by Sharpeville
nóg by die polisiestasie in Philippi
waar hy lê met 'n koeël deur sy kop

Die kind is die skaduwee van die soldate
op wag met gewere sarasene en knuppels
die kind is teenwoordig by alle vergaderings en wetgewings
die kind loer deur die vensters van huise en in die harte
    van moeders
die kind wat net wou speel in die son by Nyanga is orals
die kind wat 'n man geword het trek deur die ganse Afrika
die kind wat 'n reus geword het reis deur die hele wêreld

Sonder 'n pas

The child who was shot dead by soldiers in Nyanga
The child is not dead
the child lifts his fists against his mother
who screams Africa shouts the scent

64

of freedom and the veld
in the location of the cordoned heart

The child lifts his fists against his father
in the march of the generations
who are shouting Africa shout the scent
of righteousness and blood
in the streets of his warrior pride

The child is not dead
not at Langa not at Nyanga
not at Orlando not at Sharpeville
not at the police station in Philippi
where he lies with a bullet through his brain

The child is the shadow of the soldiers
on guard with rifles saracens and batons
the child is present at all gatherings and law-giving
the child peers through house windows and into the hearts
    of mothers
the child who just wanted to play in the sun at Nyanga is
    everywhere
The child grown to a man treks all over Africa
the child grown to a giant travels through the whole world

Without a pass

In her *Drum* article Ingrid spoke about the genesis of the poem: 'I saw the mother as every other mother in the world. I saw her as myself. I saw Simone as the baby. I could not sleep. I thought of what the child might have been had he been allowed to live. I thought what could be reached, what could be gained by death? The child wanted no part in the circumstances in which our country is grasped. He only wanted to play in the sun in Nyanga. I am not quite sure how I came to write the poem. It grew out of my poetic technique, which I have slowly developed like any workman who improves his skill by hard work. It grew out of my own experiences and sense of bereavement. It rests on a foundation of all philosophy, a certain belief in "life eternal", a belief that nothing is ever wholly lost. I am surprised when people call it political. I am warmed when others read it and thank me for it.'

By her own admission the poem has a widely universal application; on the other hand she obstinately refused, on the advice of Uys Krige, to remove those details which localised it in its specific time and place in South African history.[79] The appeal of the poem lies exactly in its combination of the very specific with the universal. Several elements in the poem must have spoken to the oppressed who became acquainted with the poem in the early 1960s: its spirit of defiance, its claim that those who died in the struggle were not dead but would live on, its assurance that the oppressed child would become a man asserting his presence in the whole of Africa and the world – in short, it was a reassurance that the struggle would not be in vain. Its final line ('Without a pass') was also a defiant stand against the apartheid laws of the time.

Jack Cope was witness to the extraordinary effect that the poem had on people: when he read it at a meeting of the Cape Night Schools' Association in June 1963, the African women in the audience wept; afterwards they swarmed up to the front to ask about the poem and copy it out.[80]

The poem's political history is well known. Oliver Tambo was the first politician to quote the poem, in his address to an international conference on 'Children, repression and the law in apartheid South Africa' in Harare on 24 September 1987.[81] Its most famous moment undoubtedly came when Nelson Mandela quoted the poem in his inaugural address to the South African parliament in 1994. On this occasion he referred to Jonker as 'an Afrikaner woman who transcended a particular experience and became a South African, an African and a citizen of the world' and cited the poem as a call for 'the liberation of the woman, the emancipation of the man and the liberty of the child' in South Africa. After this, references to the poem kept surfacing in political speeches and parliamentary debates, for instance in Thabo Mbeki's State of the Nation speeches in both 2004 and 2006.[82] Saskia van Schaik's 2002 documentary, *Korreltjie niks is my dood* [Little grain of nothing is my death], provides yet another insight into the still unfolding history of this poem. The documentary shows the Xhosa poet and teacher Sandile Dikeni visiting the sister of the boy whose killing inspired the poem, in her modest house in Nyanga East. She remembers the incident, but does not know about the poem, even after Mandela had quoted it in parliament. When she reads the final lines of the Zulu translation of the poem for the camera from the copy that Dikeni gave her, she says: 'I can't speak now, but I can understand what she is trying to say about the child.' Her eyes are luminous with unshed tears. Dikeni flees the room.

'Die kind' was not Ingrid's only response to the events in Nyanga. She also wrote an (unpublished) short story, 'Noodtoestand' [State of emergency],[83] in which the main character Marie reads about the shooting of a child in Nyanga in the newspaper and realises that the child's mother is her housekeeper. This story, which unfortunately lacks the sophistication of the poem, contrasts Marie's shocked empathy with the child's mother, with the lack of understanding shown by her sister and husband. During the first half of 1960 Ingrid also worked on 'Die bok' [The goat]. Although her passion was poetry, this was an accomplished short story which demonstrated that she had a talent for the 'open hand of prose' as well as the 'closed fist of poetry', to use Sylvia Plath's well-known comparison. 'Die bok' tells the story of a pregnant woman's disillusionment with her marriage. Her hatred of her much older husband is displaced onto the goat that destroys her rose garden. At the same time her sexual frustration and jealousy are aroused by the relationship between the servant girl Lena and her boyfriend Jager. When she wants to kill the goat with a knife, it is Jager who stops her in her tracks by commenting that the goat looks like her husband. She finally cuts the goat loose and lets him go. Although the symbolism is quite explicit, the writing is elegant and sensuous, the psychological portrait of the sexually frustrated woman precisely rendered. An English translation of the story was published in the *London Magazine* in December 1966.

Relationship with Jack Cope, psychiatric treatment
After Ingrid left her husband in January 1960 and returned to Cape Town, the close bond that already existed between her and Jack Cope gradually deepened into a romantic relationship. They lived in close proximity in Clifton and saw each other very often, going for walks, swimming in the sea, attending parties and going on outings with Jack's mother and children. At one point he commented drily in his diary: 'Had dinner with Ingrid at her new home. Her cooking is almost zero.'[84] When he was in London from the middle of April until early June 1961, she wrote to him almost daily.[85] Like the husband she had left, Jack was an older man: he was twenty years her senior and seemed able to give her the affection, stability and security she longed for. He provided practical support as well as the intellectual and literary stimulation that was so important to her. In spite of this, the relationship did not run smoothly. While she longed for a committed relationship and marriage, he was wary of marrying her. He was recently divorced and had two young sons, who

Ingrid Jonker and Jack Cope. (Courtesy of the National English Literary Museum, Grahamstown)

saw her as an unwelcome rival for their father's affections and resented her intrusion into their lives.

Not long after Jack's return from London in June 1961, Ingrid was treated in the Gardens Nursing Home after a nervous breakdown. Her fragile mental state could be attributed to a variety of factors. Her divorce from Piet Venter was not yet finalised and she had received several letters in which he threatened to take Simone from her, another reason why she was so desperate to be in a stable relationship. Her volume of poems had also been turned down for the second time by a publisher. Most important, perhaps, was the fact that she had had a backstreet abortion after becoming pregnant with Jack's child. She spoke to several people about this, telling them that Jack's unsympathetic attitude towards her pregnancy and the subsequent abortion affected her deeply. In addition, her expectation of a committed relationship was once again to be disappointed on Jack's return from England.[86] On 14 July 1961 he wrote in his diary: 'Met Ingrid at the clock & had another long inconclusive talk about a future that, to me, is non-existent.'[87] After a suicide attempt on 15 July and a breakdown, she was hospitalised in the Gardens Nursing Home more than once during the course of July and August 1961. Here she was visited by, among others, her father, who bumped into Jack on the stairs without recognising him. From this time dates another famous poem, 'Korreltjie sand' [Little grain of sand], a copy of which she gave to the psychiatrist who treated her at the time.[88] André Brink and Antjie Krog's translation follows the Afrikaans.

Korreltjie sand

Korreltjie korreltjie sand
klippie gerol in my hand
klippie gesteek in my sak
word korreltjie klein en plat

71

Sonnetjie groot in die blou
ek maak net 'n ogie van jou
blink in my korreltjie klippie
dit is genoeg vir die rukkie

Kindjie wat skreeu uit die skoot
niks in die wêreld is groot
stilletjies lag nou en praat
stilte in Doodloopstraat

Wêreldjie rond en aardblou
korreltjie maak ek van jou
huisie met deur en twee skrefies
tuintjie met blou madeliefies

Pyltjie geveer in verskiet
liefde verklein in die niet
Timmerman bou aan 'n kis
Ek maak my gereed vir die Niks

Korreltjie klein is my woord
korreltjie niks is my dood

Little grain of sand
Grain little grain of sand
pebble rolled in my hand
pebble thrust in my pocket
a keepsake for a locket

Little sun big in the blue
a granule I make out of you

72

shine in my pebble little grain
for the moment that's all I can gain

Baby that screams from the womb
nothing is big in this tomb
quietly laugh now and speak
silence in dead-end street

Little world round and earth-blue
make a mere eye out of you
house with a door and two slits
a garden where everything fits

Small arrow feathered into space
love fades away from its place
Carpenter seals a coffin that's bought
I ready myself for the nought

Small grain of sand is my word, my breath
small grain of nought is my death

The introductory image of a pebble that is picked up, rolled in the hand, put in the pocket and eventually worked into a small grain of sand can be read as a reference to the act of processing something, working it down into a small object like a grain of sand (the translation somewhat obscures this point by freely translating the first stanza's fourth line 'word korreltjie klein en plat' as 'a keepsake for a locket' in order to rhyme with 'pocket'). Taking into account the time and circumstances in which the poem was written, this image can be interpreted as an attempt at working through traumatic events and trying to reduce their harmful impact by diminishing them in size. In the second stanza the sun is made into a granule; in the third the baby that screams from the womb to be born is told that nothing in the world is big and admonished to be quiet; in the fourth the blue earth containing a little house and garden is contracted into a 'korreltjie' (the translation into English changes the 'little grain of sand' into 'a mere eye'). The fifth stanza links the disappearance of love (whether the cause or the result of the attempt to diminish the world) to the prospect of death: the carpenter is preparing the coffin and the speaker is preparing herself for the nothingness of death in the same way that she admonished the baby screaming from the womb to reconcile itself to the fact that it is in 'dead-end street'. Within this context the importance of the speaker's poetic words is diminished ('Small grain of sand is my word') as is the importance of her death ('small grain of nought is my death').

The logic of diminishment is, however, subverted by the fact that there is also something creative in this process through which certain experiences are processed and reworked into small grains or words. As such, it can be read as a metaphor for the making of meaning or the creation of artefacts such as poems that will – contrary to the overt meaning of the poem's final lines – be able to resist the nothingness and oblivion of death. Afrikaans readers will perhaps recognise a subtle reference to N.P. van Wyk Louw's iconic poem 'Die beiteltjie' [The chisel], which describes the creative process as the cleaving of a little stone that breaks the rock on which it rests and finally breaks the planet in two, resulting in a crack that runs through the stars. In Ingrid's poem the creative process is depicted as the wearing away of a little stone or pebble to create the grain-like word. Thus a poem that appears simple through its use of diminutives, tied to the traumatic circumstances of its genesis (a breakdown after an abortion), conceals unexpected resonances, demonstrating Ingrid's craft as a poet. Much has been said about the several abortions that she was supposed to have had, but none of the claims can be substantiated. That there was a termination of a pregnancy resulting from her relationship with Jack would be confirmed by a suicide note that she addressed to him shortly before her death, referring to 'that little chick of ours who has a grave in heaven'.[89]

From 1961 to 1965 Ingrid was treated by a psychiatrist, who diagnosed her as suffering from reactive depression. The psychiatrist, who later gave his impressions of Ingrid in an interview with L.M. van der Merwe, described her as very intelligent but child-like in her manner.[90] He did not judge her to be either manic-depressive or psychotic and felt that her depression was caused by adverse circumstances: her traumatic childhood, her unhappy marriage, unsatisfactory sexual relationships, financial problems, her job and other general frustrations that often left her desperate, not knowing which way to turn. Despite the tendency to depression and anxiety, Ingrid's friends also remembered her as someone with a tremendous capacity for fun, gaiety and laughter. She was an intensely sociable person who needed the company of others to survive and was happiest when she was with other people, as she once admitted in an interview. She was open about her feelings and passionate in her convictions, unable to make compromises about those values she found important.

As circumstances began to weigh on her, her behaviour became increasingly volatile and difficult for others to deal with. Periods of elfin charm and emotional calm alternated with bouts of extreme anxiety and tension, which led to drinking and an excessive use of medication. Generosity and loyalty towards her friends alternated with selfishness and a childish need for attention and affirmation. She herself would later laughingly admit that her temperament as an artist made her petulant and demanding to such a degree that she would throw a tantrum if she could not have her way.[91] Moments of intense self-doubt were followed by self-aggrandisement, as both Jack Cope and her friend Bonnie Davidtsz commented.[92] On one hand, she had almost impossibly high standards of truthfulness and integrity; on the other hand, friends recalled that she increasingly lost touch with reality, sometimes weaving webs of lies and obfuscations.

Although she was completely comfortable with her own physicality and confident in her sensuality, she had a constant need to have her beauty and attractiveness confirmed. More than once she asked lovers or friends whether they still thought her body beautiful. Her obsession with mirrors indicated a further need to have her very existence affirmed by external means. What André Brink would call her 'quicksilvery changes of mood'[93] added to her immense attraction for both men and women, but also made her demanding and difficult to be with. There was a restlessness that was difficult to ease: Marjorie Wallace remembered that after she was released from hospital, painting her portrait was the only way of getting her to sit still in one place. Added to the feeling of despair caused by difficult circumstances, there also seems to have been an infatuation with death, so that she repeatedly tried to commit suicide. On one hand, it seemed like a macabre game with death that fascinated her endlessly. André Brink commented that she regarded her own suicide as a given and that her remarks about it were often uttered matter-of-factly, even lightheartedly.[94] On the other hand, repeated attempts at suicide often spring from the individual's feeling of being worthless; being saved affirms the sense of self-worth and the feeling of being important to others. In Ingrid's case this happened so often that her friends later became indifferent to her cries for help.

That she possessed insight into her own mental state is clear from the fact that she sought psychiatric help when she was under strain. When she had herself admitted to Valkenburg from 21 to 28 April 1962 she wrote on the admission form: 'My reason for seeking admission is nervous disorder, anxiety and depression'.[95] Over the years she would be treated in psychiatric hospitals like Valkenburg and the Gardens Nursing Home. Doctors would use anti-depressive medication as well as shock therapy to treat her. In addition to individual therapy she attended group sessions conducted by her psychiatrist, who also saw her and Jack together in an attempt to solve their relationship problems. Although Jack was unwilling to marry her, he would not be able to disentangle his life emotionally from hers in the years that followed, even though there were other women in his life. A diary entry on 6 June 1964 indicates that his feelings for her had by that time developed into a tortured love–hate relationship. On that day he wrote: 'Rain – I walked & thought of all that is so impure. Ingrid – thee I love, and thee I hate.'

5

Prize-winning poet, 1963–1964

> *'We are and have been fighting for freedom of*
> *expression in our country and we, as writers, will*
> *never come to terms with the enemy.'*
> *– Ingrid Jonker in letter to the* Sunday Times,
> *August 1963*

Political involvement

There is a tendency to emphasise Ingrid Jonker's sexuality, her vulnerability, her artistic talent and emotional volatility to such a degree that her interest in the politics of the day is underestimated. In his 1982 book on dissident Afrikaans writers, *The adversary within,* Jack Cope wrote that she was 'non-political in any party or local sense', that she 'at no time intentionally wrote a *political* poem' and was not 'committed or *engagé* in the usual drift of current clichés'.[96] Although Ingrid was never a political activist, she abhorred the injustices of apartheid. The story is told of her attacking a bus conductor who pushed a coloured passenger off a bus.[97] Her friend Berta Smit also remembered that she would often express her dismay at the daily newspapers' reports of incidents of racial discrimination.[98] Her letters to friends not only focused on personal and literary matters, but also responded to the political events of the day. Letters written from Johannesburg in the late 1950s are critical of Verwoerd and the racial attitudes of whites, while those she wrote almost daily to Jack while he was in London in 1961 commented on South Africa's forthcoming withdrawal from the Commonwealth, the political tension and threatened strike during the build-up to Republic Day on 31 May, parliament's passing of the 'Lock-up Bill', which would enable police to detain any person without trial or bail for 12 days, the banning of meetings and gatherings until 26 June and the arrest of thousands of people. She also shared her feelings of general foreboding about the future of South Africa.[99]

Ingrid was also involved in protests against censorship, which brought her into direct confrontation with her father's political views. In 1956 the Cronjé Commission on Censorship proposed a harsh set of recommendations that would regulate all publications. In the years that followed, Abraham Jonker became a vocal supporter of censorship in parliamentary debates, apparently in the hope that he would be appointed chairman of the proposed Board of Censors. The dreaded Publications and Entertainment Act was eventually signed into law in March 1963. It comprised 'five main clauses, covering what could be deemed morally repugnant, blasphemous, socially subversive and politically seditious,' writes Peter McDonald in *The literature police.*[100] A petition against the censorship laws, largely drafted by Jan Rabie, was signed by 133 writers and 58 artists and handed to the Minister of the Interior on 25 April 1963 by the writers Mary Renault, then president of PEN SA, and W.A. (Bill) de Klerk.[101] By that time the law was already a *fait accompli*. Although the petition succeeded in uniting South African writers across a broader front than before, Es'kia Mphahlele pointed out that it was compromised by its omission of many African writers (only five of the signatories were not white: Richard Rive, James Matthews, S.V. Petersen, P.J. (Piet) Philander and Adam Small).[102]

Ingrid took an active part in the campaign against censorship, not only by signing the petition but also by helping to collect signatures. The hostility between Ingrid and her father on this point was eagerly fanned by newspaper reporters. The *Sunday Times* of 26 May 1963 reported that Ingrid had responded angrily when told that her father dismissed the writers who signed the petition as 'nobodies', retorting that his statement was 'ridiculous'. The headline 'Dad was "ridiculous", says Ingrid Jonker' was almost guaranteed to sour relations with her father. The question of censorship also cropped up in Ingrid's article for *Drum* in May 1963 in which she wrote: 'Controversies rage in the press. Poets and writers are not politicians or legislators, but they find it necessary to speak according to their conscience without control or interference.' A few months later, in August 1963, she followed this up with a letter to the *Sunday Times* in which she again protested against the censorship law: 'Attempts to intimidate and victimise thinking people in all professions are being made, and have been made, especially in the past few months. Alarm and despondency, particularly among writers, has been aroused – and censorship has now become a fact. A play and also a novel by South African writers have been banned by the Publications Control Board in the past eight weeks. A foremost and highly regarded South African professor and Afrikaans poet [N.P. van Wyk Louw] has recently surprised the South African literary world by a vicious and personal attack on the integrity of certain English-speaking writers in South Africa. A new enemy now seems to have emerged against our writers. It is now possible that they can be tarred, feathered and silenced even before censorship. This was the case with André Brink whose novel *Orgie* was withdrawn by the publishers after the page proofs had been passed. We are and have been fighting for freedom of expression in our country and we, as writers, will never come to terms with the enemy.'[103] In this way Ingrid took a stand against censorship, professed her solidarity with all South African writers, not only Afrikaans ones, in the face of the influential Louw, criticised pre-publication censorship and courageously termed the law-makers of the country (among them her father) 'the enemy'. In a radio interview conducted in November 1964 she also made a plea for poems in Afrikaans that would deal frankly with the country's racial problems.[104]

Relationship with André Brink

The petition against censorship brought Ingrid into contact for the first time with André Brink, the young writer and spokesman for the Sestigers. Brink, who was a married man and a lecturer in Afrikaans at Rhodes University in Grahamstown at the time, visited Cape Town in April 1963 to see Jan Rabie about the petition. It was here that he first met Ingrid in the company of several other writers, among them Jack Cope. He later recalled the electricity in the air when he saw her for the first time in tight-fitting pants and with bare feet. She and Jack were constantly taking opposite viewpoints, Ingrid with such passion and conviction that she made an immediate impression on Brink.[105] Her relationship with Jack had run into troubled waters by this time and Ingrid had taken refuge in a relationship with the artist Nico Hagen. When she met Brink she was extremely despondent and on the verge of suicide after the break-up of the relationship with Hagen. There was an immediate rapport between Ingrid and André and the meeting would be the start of a stormy love affair. Brink later wrote in his memoir *A fork in the road* that he found her to be the 'living incarnation' of the character Nicolette in *Die ambassadeur* [The ambassador], the novel he had

Etienne Leroux, Ingrid Jonker, Jan Rabie, Marjorie Wallace and André Brink. (Jan Rabie & Marjorie Wallace collection, UWC)

finished writing shortly before meeting her. He even had time to flesh out the character by adding a few references to Ingrid before the novel was published later in 1963. While the relationship lasted, Brink commuted between his home in Grahamstown and Cape Town to see Ingrid in romantic hide-outs in Stellenbosch, Franschhoek, Gordon's Bay and Hout Bay.

During the next two years a peculiar and destructive triangular relationship developed between Ingrid, Jack and André. Although Brink quoted Ingrid in his memoir as saying that his appearance on the scene rekindled Jack's romantic interest in her and even made him mention marriage for the first time,[106] she received a letter from Jack two months after first meeting André in which he broke off their relationship. This did not, however, bring an end to all contact between Jack and Ingrid. Whenever André appeared on the scene Jack would become jealously possessive: there are tales of a party at Bill de Klerk's where he caused a scene on seeing them together.[107] And once André left, Jack would lose interest. In her turn Ingrid kept wavering between the two men: when André left for Grahamstown, returning to his wife, she turned to Jack, only to leave him when André reappeared.[108] The lasting commitment to marriage that Ingrid craved was not to be forthcoming from either of them. Although there were other men in her life, her relationship with these two writers seems to have been a determining factor in her final years. They shared her passion for literature and both inspired her to write poetry; sometimes she would dedicate and send the same poem to the two, arousing considerable irritation and jealousy in each.

Part of one's understanding of Ingrid Jonker as a person no doubt involves grasping something of her sexual appeal, her physical attraction for both men and women. In this respect, one has to rely on the reactions of others, although only a few have expressed themselves in writing. The whole of André Brink's impressive oeuvre bears testimony to the emotional, physical and sexual impact Ingrid had on those closely involved with her. He writes in *A fork in the road* that 'this small person with her large eyes and unkempt hair' would affect the way in which he constructed female characters in his novels, influence his notions of plot and determine his involvement with other people for the rest of his life.[109] Trying to understand her attraction for his father, Jack's son Michael writes in *Intricacy*: 'She brought with her the atmosphere of emotional turmoil, distress and physical chaos that drove her repeatedly into the sea or to the bottle of pills, and eventually killed her. At the same time she was clever, articulate, sexy, dangerous and unrequited but full of desire – qualities that made her, as I reconstruct it, a flame to the moth of various men, including my father.'[110] One finds an oblique sense of her attraction for women, filtered through the refracting lens of fiction, in a novel by Berta Smit, a close female friend.[111] In this novel, *Die vrou en die bees* [The woman and the beast], published in 1964, Smit created a female character called Julia who shares many characteristics with the biographical Ingrid. This largely allegorical work emphasises Julia's youthfulness, her spontaneity, her ability to bind people to her, her physical beauty and attraction for men, her love of the sea and the beach. The novel also includes references to a drowning that Julia witnesses on the beach – echoing an experience of Ingrid and her sister Anna when they were young children.[112]

The publication of *Rook en oker*

The year 1963 also saw the publication of Ingrid's second volume, *Rook en oker* [Smoke and ochre], in October. It was this volume that established her reputation as a poet in Afrikaans. The film *Black butterflies* suggests that the collection was compiled by Jack Cope and Uys Krige after Jack found the poems in her handbag, which was given to him when he visited her in hospital at Valkenburg. This version of events reinforces a rather insidious image of Ingrid as the stereotypical female hysteric and paints her as a purely intuitive writer who had flashes of brilliance but could not rationally structure her own work without male guidance. Nothing could be further from the truth. Ingrid's letters to Uys reveal that she was constantly working on her poems, trying to refine and improve them. She also mentioned the possibility of a second volume in a letter to Uys as early as December 1959.[113] At that point she felt that it was high time for a new collection, as three years had elapsed since the publication of *Ontvlugting*. Shortly before leaving Johannesburg at the beginning of 1960 she sent an untitled volume to the publisher Gerry de Melker at HAUM, who asked the poet D.J. Opperman for a reader's report. Opperman felt that the volume did not do justice to her talent and advised against its publication. A revised version of the volume, now titled *Ukulele*, was turned down by both Ernst Lindenberg and Opperman in March 1961. When Ingrid wanted to discuss Opperman's report with him,

87

he invited her to make an appointment with him but she seemed (wrongly) to interpret it as a refusal to see her. 'What do you think of Opperman not wanting to speak to me? I find it a rather strange reflection on his character,' she wrote to Jack in May 1961.[114]

The volume was finally accepted for publication by Afrikaanse Pers Boekhandel (APB), where Bartho Smit was the publisher and where he championed the work of Sestigers like Chris Barnard, Breyten Breytenbach, Jan Rabie and Adam Small. Smit's enthusiasm for their work was constrained by the firm's conservative nature – it had Prime Minister Verwoerd as chairman of its board of directors.[115] Ingrid resisted attempts to get her to omit the poem 'Die kind' from *Rook en oker*. Smit wrote in his memoir that although there were reservations about including the poem in the volume, his boss Willem van Heerden managed to dissuade Verwoerd from excluding it.[116] Jack Cope gave a different version of events, according to which Bartho Smit flew to Cape Town from Johannesburg with the instruction to persuade Ingrid to remove the poems 'Die kind' and 'Madeliefies in Namakwaland' [Daisies in Namaqualand]. It was either that or they would refuse to publish the book. After taking legal opinion, she refused and both poems were eventually included in the volume.[117] Ingrid later told the journalist Aletta Greyling that she had threatened to withdraw the volume when Smit informed her that he wanted to submit the book to the board of directors for approval.[118]

'Die kind' was, however, placed in the volume's fourth section, consisting mostly of poems for children. In the second edition of the volume the poems were rearranged and 'Die kind' was moved to the final section, but it still appeared under its abbreviated title 'Die Kind', which lessened the impact of its reference to the events of 1960. The full title was restored in *Seismograph*, a collection of the best writings from *Contrast*, in 1970 and was also used in the 1994 edition of Ingrid's *Versamelde werke*, edited by her sister Anna.

Although publication of *Rook en oker* was delayed by technical problems with the first printing, it finally appeared in October 1963. Uys Krige's mentorship was clearly visible: exposure to his critical eye ensured that the poems were finely crafted and, thanks to his introducing her to surrealist poets like Paul Éluard, her style became more supple. She now wrote free verse instead of the rhyming couplets of her first volume and used the disarming images associated with surrealism. It was also clear that her extensive reading of other poets had made her poetry more sophisticated without detracting from its freshness.

The volume was divided into five sections on the basis of content and form, the arrangement of poems finding its proper shape only in the rearranged second edition. The poems in the first section focus on the body in relationship to others, the lover, the self, the unborn child, with the poem 'Swanger vrou' [Pregnant woman] finding

Ingrid Jonker (cradling Simone) and Uys Krige at Cape Point.
(Courtesy of the National English Literary Museum, Grahamstown)

its place in this section. Especially evocative is the poem
'Ek herhaal jou' [I repeat you] in which details of time and
place fade into the background in the face of the speaker's
intense bodily involvement with the lover. She 'repeats'

him because the contours of her body are determined by his: her breasts are a repetition of the hollows of his hands. In an Esscher-like loop of interdependence and repetition 'without beginning or end' it is not clear where the one ends and the other begins, as can be seen in the Afrikaans original and its translation by André Brink and Antjie Krog:

Ek herhaal jou
Ek herhaal jou
sonder begin of einde
herhaal ek jou liggaam
Die dag het 'n smal skadu
en die nag geel kruise
die landskap is sonder aansien
en die mense 'n ry kerse
terwyl ek jou herhaal
met my borste
wat die holtes van jou hande namaak

I repeat you
I repeat you
without beginning or end
repeat your body
The day has a thin shadow
the night yellow crosses
the landscape has no distinction
and the people a row of candles

while I repeat you
with my breasts
which imitate the hollow of your hands

The second section, entitled 'Intimate conversation', consists of short poems presenting flash-like images ('Your body is / heavy with blood / and your back / a singing guitar'), ostensibly addressed to a lover, describing aspects of his body and being. These fragments actually come from the play *'n Seun na my hart*, written in 1959, in which these images are used by the deluded mother either to address or describe her imaginary son. The songs in the third section come closest to the rhythmical patterns of her first volume but bring variation by adopting the voices and speech patterns of other characters (a troubadour, a coloured man), frequently expressing dismay about the loss of love and the bitterness of betrayal. The most expressive of these poems is the haunting 'Bitterbessie dagbreek' [Bitter-berry daybreak] in which the bitterness of love's loss is amplified by the imagery and taunting, echoing rhymes. The volume also includes a section with poems for and about children, among them 'Begin somer' [Early summer], 'Kabouterliefde' [Pixie love] and 'Toemaar die donker man' [Hush now the darkling man] dedicated to Simone. The first is a celebration of summer in which the child plays the sun like a ukulele all day long; the last is a dark lullaby in which the reader gradually becomes aware that the 'darkling man' ('donker man') with the name Hush Now ('Toemaar' in Afrikaans) refers not only to the approaching sleep but also death. Somewhat inappropriately, the darkly ambiguous poem 'Korreltjie sand' [Little grain of sand] is included in the section of poems for children, both in the first and second editions.

The poems in the final section acknowledge that the poet lives in a materialistic, destructive, violent and torn society, but still reach out towards a life of freedom, generosity and connectedness. In 'Die kind' (moved here in the second edition) there is the confident assertion that the child will be able to break out of his constraints to become a man striding the world. In 'Gesien uit die wond in my sy' [Seen from the wound in my side] the Christ figure looks down on his own body, broken by those he came to redeem, but finds hope in his disciple John's gesture of reaching out to the black man carrying the cross. In 'Madeliefies in Namakwaland' [Daisies in Namaqualand] the speaker feels there is still some form of hope despite all the destructive features of a 'land torn apart': in this poem she finds it in the language of the veld ('dazed we still hear / small blue Namaqualand daisy / answering something, believing something, knowing something'). The final poem in the volume, 'L'art poetique' [The art of poetry], gives a telling indication of how poetry had come to function for Ingrid: as a hiding-place, a space in which she can stow herself away in her words. *Rook en oker* marks the emergence of Ingrid's following in the Afrikaans literary world: in the immediate years that followed, her poems would be anthologised and several academic articles and theses would be devoted to her work.

APB prize and overseas trip

When *Rook en oker* was published, Ingrid wanted to present her father with a copy of the book at a meeting in a restaurant, possibly in an attempt to reassure herself that he was prepared to acknowledge her publicly as his daughter. Once more it seems that it was difficult for Abraham Jonker to concede that his daughter had achieved something in a field in which he himself had had only moderate success. It is also possible that her open defiance of him in the press still rankled. Though his reaction was perhaps to be expected, it still hurt her deeply. When she tried to organise a meeting, he responded with a letter on 7 January 1964 which she quoted in a letter to André Brink:[119] 'Dear Ingrid, After what you have done to me in your interviews with *The Sunday Times* and other papers in the past year, I do not feel inclined to meet you in a restaurant or any other public place. If you want to discuss something with me, you know where I live. All that you have to do is to phone me and enquire whether the time is convenient. On weekend afternoons I usually go fishing. With love from Daddy, Abraham H. Jonker' [my translation]. Ingrid's outraged reaction also remains preserved in her letter to Brink: 'How and where and why did it all begin? The injury, mostly in secret. And then he really thinks that I who am not allowed to meet him in public will do it in secret! Not on an equal footing, not as person to person, let alone as daughter to father. And to what end? Where does the pettiness and the decay and the narrow-mindedness and the parochialism and bitterness and closedness start? Where does it end?' [my translation]. Her indignant reaction hints at a deep-seated hurt and an inability to fathom the motive for her father's unyielding attitude.

The critics wrote enthusiastic reviews of the book and in 1964 it was awarded the APB prize for the best Afrikaans book published in 1963. The prize, worth the substantial amount of R2000, had been set up to improve the image of APB and attract new writers. The judges were the academic worthies Ernst van Heerden, Rob Antonissen and D.J. Opperman, who chose the book over contenders like Jan Rabie's novel *Mens-alleen.* Opperman, who had rejected earlier versions for publication, was now favourably impressed with the way in which Ingrid had revised it and added new poems.[120] After hearing the news of the prize, Ingrid again contacted her father. She asked him to accompany her to the prize-giving ceremony on 28 February 1964 in Johannesburg, offering to pay for his air-ticket, but he refused.[121] The publication of *Rook en oker* and the prize it won led to even more public exposure for Ingrid, who was already known in the public mind as the liberally minded, poetry-writing daughter of the

National Party MP Abraham Jonker. She now came into her own right as a prize-winning poet. She was written about and interviewed on the radio and in newspapers. Despite her disappointment about the uncompromising attitude of her father, these interviews radiate excitement and self-confidence.

Ingrid was now able to realise the long-held dream of going overseas. In interviews she told of her wish to study poetry in Amsterdam, an ideal she had pursued once before by enquiring about bursaries for young poets at the Cultural Desk of the Dutch Embassy in Pretoria at the end of 1963. The APB prize money now made it possible for her to plan an overseas trip. To this she was later able to add a bursary of R500 awarded by the Anglo American Corporation in April 1964.[122] Simone was to stay with Piet and his new wife Topsi while Ingrid was overseas. Barely a month after receiving the prize, Ingrid left Cape Town for England on the *Windsor Castle*. She was extremely anxious and nervous in the build-up to the trip, foreseeing all kinds of problems. Jack helped her with her preparations and, after a 'last happy night together', as he noted in his diary, saw her off on 27 March with a bouquet of flowers on board the ship. She was interviewed by a reporter from the *Cape Times* and friends like Richard Rive and Alf Wannenburgh also came to say goodbye. Jack wrote to his London friends Doris Lessing, John St John, William Plomer, Enslin du Plessis, Pat and Peggy Cope and David Lytton that she was coming. On board ship she

Ingrid Jonker accepting the APB Prize, 1964, with Ernst van Heerden, Rob Antonissen, D.J. Opperman and (in front) Simone. (Courtesy of the National Afrikaans Literary Museum and Research Centre)

met Laurens van der Post, who was very much taken with her. He would afterwards be very critical of the role that both Jack and André played in her life. He promised to introduce her to the literary world in London and would later try to help her in various ways when circumstances became difficult during the trip. David Lytton met her shortly after her arrival in London and took her to stay with him in Stratford-on-Avon. He wrote to their mutual friends in Cape Town that she was spending money wildly and seemed emotionally unprepared for the trip to Europe that lay ahead. He would later describe her visit in the piece 'Ingrid comes to Stratford', published in *Contrast* in April 1967, remembering her mood swings and references to suicide.

From the outset the trip did not fulfil her expectations. David Lytton commented that she could not find a connection with either London or the English countryside and felt a constant nostalgia for South Africa. From England she travelled to Amsterdam, which did not live up to her expectations either. The meetings with Dutch writers did not seem to materialise. To Jan and Marjorie she wrote that they would be glad to hear she was not meeting any artists (she mockingly used the word 'artieste' to speak to their horror of pomposity) and was making herself at home among ordinary people.[123] She returned to England for a short while before going back to Amsterdam to wait for André, whom she had arranged to meet there in June. He had been commissioned by his Cape Town publisher to write a travel book on Spain and they planned to travel to Paris, before going on to Spain. Just how unbearably fraught with tension her emotional life had become by that time is revealed when one pieces together the narrative from the little currently available of the correspondence between Jack and Ingrid and between André and Ingrid. It is possible that her anxiety and depression can be attributed to the emotional insecurity caused by the complexity of her relationships with the two men. She was corresponding with both while she was in Europe as well as writing poems that she sometimes sent to both of them. From the time in Amsterdam dates the poem 'Wagtyd in Amsterdam' [Waiting in Amsterdam], of which she sent copies to both Jack and André, each with a dedication to its receiver. The poem is a haunting expression of disappointed longing for the lover who turns aside to go his own way on his long-awaited arrival. The final lines read (in a translation by Brink and Krog):

> jy het jou voël afgehaal
> dit op die tafel neergelê
> en sonder om te praat
> met jou eie glimlag
> die wêreld verlaat

> [but unperturbed you turned your back
> you took off your cock
> laid it on the table
> and without a word
> with your own smile
> forsook the world]

The correspondence between Ingrid and Jack (as reported by Johan van Wyk, who had access to the documents, in his book *Gesig van die liefde*)[124] shows that Jack was dismayed to discover that the relationship with André was not over. His letters to her became subtly undermining of her confidence ('People are beginning to say you are overrated, that you won't do better than *Rook en oker* & that you have a swelled head. Don't worry about that either – every real writer gets more kicks than ha'pence,' he wrote on 26 May 1964). He also expressed his irritation about a love poem dedicated to André that was published in the journal *Sestiger*. The letter referred as well to a phone call on his birthday in which Ingrid threatened to go to Paris with André if Jack did not promise to marry her. In a later letter he indicated that he was not at all impressed with the poem 'Wagtyd in Amsterdam', saying that he found the final lines 'flat and toneless' and that the use of the word 'voël' [cock] made it unsuitable for publication in South Africa. In his diary he wrote that the poem 'is good most of the way but has a faulty phallic or surrealist ending'.[125] The poem's reference to the male sexual organ was, however, in keeping with the forthright style of Ingrid's poetry and was no more provocative than writing by other Sestigers like Breytenbach and Brink. On 17 June Ingrid again wrote to Jack and presented an ultimatum that should he not undertake to marry her, she would go to Paris with André. On receiving this letter five days later, Jack wrote in his diary: 'Then thrown into a raging pit by a false-tongued letter from Ingrid. Off to France for her rendezvous with André Brink & tries to blame me for this. So this is goodbye. Goodbye to the heartache, & the wonder, the lies & posing, goodbye to all the past & the future, goodbye to dreams & memories, goodbye forever.'

André arrived in Amsterdam on 20 June. He and Ingrid spent a few days in Amsterdam before leaving for Paris, where they met up with Breyten Breytenbach and his Vietnamese wife Yolande. Although Ingrid had known Breyten from the late 1950s when he was still a student, it was André's first meeting with him. André later remembered that there was no feeling of rivalry between the two poets.[126] Ingrid was the established poet who had just won the APB prize; Breyten was the debut poet who had just published his innovative first volume, *Die ysterkoei moet sweet* [The iron cow must sweat] (for which, incidentally, he would win the same prize in the following year). Ingrid was excited to have André with her and wanted to celebrate his arrival with drinks and dinners; his feelings of guilt about cheating on his wife were compounded by his worries that all the partying would tax his limited budget. Although they were both charmed by Paris, the cracks started to show during their short stay there from 22 to 26 June. Things finally came to a head in Barcelona, where André had to meet with Spanish publishers on behalf of his Cape Town publisher and Ingrid reproached him for neglecting her. After several rows it was decided that Ingrid should return to Paris and try to salvage something of her European trip, while staying with Breyten and Yolande.

Ingrid's diary gives her own cryptic version of the few days she spent in Barcelona. On their arrival in the city on 27 June, she wrote: 'Vernederd' [Humiliated]. On 28 June things had lightened up slightly because they visited the cathedral and attended a bullfight. On 29 June she wrote 'Finale', noting that she had had to cancel her flight to Paris because she had a breakdown at the airport. They returned to the hotel. She then left for Paris on 30 June after only four days in Spain. Her diary entry concluded: 'Vaarwel, André P. Brink, if it must be' [Farewell, André P. Brink, if it must be]. It is clear from other entries in her diary, shown to a journalist by Anna Jonker,[127] that these events left her with an overwhelming feeling of humiliation, inadequacy and fear. She felt she had become a burden to André, who did not want her any more, and wondered desperately how in these circumstances she could save herself. Even though this sounds like a tale of utter despair and despondency, she managed to sound optimistic in a letter that she wrote to Jack on 27 June from Barcelona, telling him about her plans to settle in Paris because she thought that the city exuded 'the necessary emotional climate for writing'.

Ingrid was, however, extremely depressed when she arrived in Paris to stay with Breyten and his wife Yolande. Eventually things got so bad that she felt she had to get psychiatric treatment. Breyten took her to David and Evalda Matthews, South African friends who lived close by. They tried to dissuade her from going to the mental hospital St Anne because they'd heard that once one went in there, one never came out. But Ingrid insisted and they took her to St Anne's, where she was admitted in the early hours of Saturday 4 July. When the staff heard she was a poet, their attitude towards her changed from surly to almost reverent.[128] She was eventually discharged on 12 July and flew back to South Africa on the same day, wearing the nightdress that André had bought for her in Paris and a green cashmere coat, which was a present from Laurens van der Post. Even though her friend Lena Oelofse recalled that Ingrid was in a good mood when she arrived in Cape Town ('totally the old Ingrid, very normal and jolly'),[129] the abrupt termination of her 'year in Europe' left her with a sense of failure.

The days shortly before and after her return to South Africa yielded a number of poems in which she evaluated her relationship with André Brink, expressed her feeling of destitution and also wondered about the reception awaiting her in Cape Town.[130] While still in Paris she wrote a farewell poem to Brink, 'Reis om die wêreld vir André' [Journey around the world for André], recalling both the tender and bitter moments of their time together and concluding with the injunction 'gaan héén / bevrug die aarde' [go forth / impregnate the earth]. The poem 'Mamma' also dates from this time and expresses an overwhelming sense of futility and the loss of identity: 'mamma is nie meer 'n mens nie / net 'n 'n' [mommy is no longer a person / just an a].[131] She also wrote two versions of the poem 'Heimwee na Kaapstad' [Nostalgia for Cape Town].[132] In the first she longs for the city of Cape Town, sure that it will protect her like a mother even though she does not know that her child is hungry, scared and dying of the 'galloping consumption' caused by love. A few days later she wrote a parody on this poem in which the mother city wants to cut her throat and

103

place her under house arrest. Though the second version was never published, a comparison between the two reveals something of her uncertainty about the welcome awaiting her in Cape Town. Both poems expressed not only a longing to return to Cape Town, but also the fear that she would not be unconditionally accepted by the city and all it represented: her country, her family, her friends, her lover Jack.

As letters from this period show, Ingrid's fears about her return were indeed warranted, as far as her relationship with Jack was concerned. Though she tried to restore relations, he remained distant, not able to forgive her for having an affair with André and meeting him in Paris. She wrote to him on 25 July after spending a day with him and his children on Table Mountain, declaring her love and stating that she had returned to South Africa to be with him.[133] The image of an 'emotional slaughterhouse', which surfaced in more than one of her letters at the time, gives an indication of her state of mind shortly after her return. In August she wrote to Laurens van der Post, telling him that her emotional despair was being compounded by the political situation in the country. On the one hand there was the 'nederlaag' [defeat] of her European tour and the failure of her relationships with both Jack and André. On the other hand intellectuals were being arrested and the books of writers refused publication without explanation or compensation. 'I'm losing heart,' she concluded, a little less than a year before

Ingrid Jonker. (Courtesy of the National English Literary Museum, Grahamstown)

her suicide. In other correspondence she said that she wanted to return to Paris, hoping that she would be able to study French at the Sorbonne. In order to support herself, she worked as a translator for the Cape Divisional Council in the five months following her return from Europe. To earn money she also translated a children's book by the German-American author Margret Vogel, *The don't be scared book,* into Afrikaans as *Moenie skrik nie.* She wrote very little poetry during this time, although there were negotiations about the inclusion of some poems in Opperman's anthology *Groot verseboek* and the translation of others into German. Her publisher Bartho Smit was also busy preparing a third volume of her poetry, provisionally entitled *Windroos* [Wind rose], for which he sent her a contract in November 1964.[134]

Although there was little communication between Ingrid and André after their separation in Barcelona, he again saw her in Cape Town in the middle of December. The end of this visit was marked by a huge row and an attempt by Ingrid to throw herself under a car. After this stormy episode she wrote him a sweetly idealistic poem about an idyllic life together, 'Plant vir my 'n boom André' [Plant me a tree André].[135] She continued to write to him after he left to be with his family in Grahamstown. The destructive pattern of their relationship resumed: intimacy followed by bewildering distance. It seems that being close to Ingrid was irresistible for both André and Jack, but they were fearful of a lasting commitment because of her emotional intensity. She spent Christmas of 1964 alone: Simone was still with her father in Johannesburg, André was with his family in Grahamstown and Jack on the Cope family farm in Natal. Over the New Year she attended what she termed 'a decadent party' where she lashed out when some of the Afrikaner nationalists present criticised her for 'Die kind' and made disparaging remarks about Jews. All in all, she wrote to her friend Bonnie, the New Year had had a 'shitty' start for her and most of the people she knew.[136] It was to be the year in which she finally succumbed to the ever-present urge to commit suicide.

6

Last days, 1965

'A suicide kills two people, Maggie, that's what it's for.'

— *Arthur Miller*, After the fall

Plans to leave Cape Town

By the beginning of 1965 Ingrid thought that her relationship with André Brink was secure. It was in fact the one thing that gave her some hope in an otherwise bleak start to the new year. On 6 January she was taken to hospital by Jack after she suffered an anxiety attack while at work, followed by a loss of consciousness for three hours. To André she wrote that the attack had been caused by a fear of Jack and a fear of loneliness, concluding with the hope that she would one day be able to live a normal life with him. To her friend Bonnie she phrased it somewhat differently, saying that the attack was caused by a fear of Jack, of herself, of 'guilt'. Here she acknowledged that her anxiety was possibly caused by the feeling she had betrayed Jack and failed to meet her own expectations and those of others about her

European trip. Ingrid came to the conclusion that she had to leave Cape Town and settle in Johannesburg. Simone was still with her father and Ingrid planned to fetch her when she had a job and a place to live in Johannesburg. She was tired of the Clifton group and the gossiping, she wrote. Her old friends were not sympathetic any more. Uys was irritated with her and the tension between Jack and her drove their mutual friends into different camps. When the one was invited to a party, the other could not come, and so on. The heady and inspiring Clifton days, it seemed, were over.

Two poems that date from this time (included in the posthumously published *Kantelson*) show that her highly strung nervous state was not only the result of her relationship problems and her increasing estrangement from her Clifton circle of friends, but also of a general unease about the country's politics. She wrote the poems 'Met hulle is ek' [I am with those] and 'Ek dryf in die wind' [I drift in the wind] in January 1965. An unusual bitterness is voiced in 'Met hulle is ek', translated by Ingrid herself as 'I am with those'.

I am with those
I am with those
who abuse sex
because the individual doesn't count
with those who get drunk
against the abyss of the brain

against the illusion that life
had once been beautiful or good or sacred
against the garden parties of falseness
against the silence beating at the temples
with those who poor and old
race against death the atom bomb of the days
with those stupefied in institutions
shocked with electric currents
through the cataracts of the senses
with those whose hearts have been removed
like the light from the robot of safety
with those coloured african deprived
with those who kill
because every death confirms anew
the lie of life
and please forget
about justice   it doesn't exist
about brotherhood   it's deceit
about love   it has no right

The speaker in this poem boldly identifies herself with the immoral (those who abuse sex, those who kill), the undisciplined (those who get drunk), the deprived (the poor, the old, the mentally ill who are stupefied by shock treatment), the cold-blooded (those whose hearts have been removed) and those without rights (coloureds and africans). The poem's conclusion speaks of utter disillusion: justice does not exist, brotherhood is a deception, love has no right to exist in the world the speaker inhabits. The sentiment in this poem stands in stark contrast with the defiant optimism so strongly in evidence in a poem like 'Die kind'.

An even stronger indictment of South African society can be found in the poem 'Ek dryf in die wind' [I drift in the wind] of which several manuscript versions exist, one with the title 'Suid-Afrika 1965' [South Africa 1965].[137] The speaker in the poem refers to all those who have forsaken her: her friends, her mother and father, her landscape, her nation. Jack Cope and William Plomer's translation of the poem concludes with the lines:[138]

My people have rotted away from me
what will become of the rotten nation
a hand cannot pray alone

The sun will cover us
the sun in our eyes covered for ever
with black crows

An alternative translation by André Brink and Antjie Krog, based on another manuscript version of the poem, ends with a different image:[139]

My volk has rotted away from me
what will become of this rotted volk
a hand cannot pray on its own

111

The sun shall be covered by us
the sun in our eyes for ever covered
with black butterflies

The most striking difference between the two versions is that
the image of the 'black crows' in the first version is replaced
by that of 'black butterflies' in the second. The image of
'black crows' hints at destruction and ruin; visually, it
also reminds one of Van Gogh's painting 'Wheatfield with
crows', a reading that is confirmed by Ingrid calling it her
'Van Gogh poem' in a letter to Bonnie.[140] The image of the
'black butterflies', on the other hand, is more ambivalent
although the context prompts one to read it as a reference
to a beautifully fragile form of life which is unexpectedly
described as having the ability to block out the sun. The
same image is used in the deeply melancholic poem 'As
jy weer skryf' [When you write again], dedicated to Jack,
in which the speaker also refers to the fact that she has
covered the sun in her eyes with black butterflies. Such is
the evocative power of the image that Brink and Krog chose
it as the title for their selection of poems in translation
from Jonker's oeuvre and Dutch film-maker Paula van der
Oest also used it as the title of her 2011 film about Jonker.
Although one must be wary of using fictional constructs
such as poems as evidence of what happened in Ingrid's
life, these poems may very well indicate her state of mind at
the beginning of 1965. She felt forsaken by her friends, cut
off from her family and her fellow Afrikaners.

The end of the relationship with André Brink

By the middle of January, Simone was back with Ingrid in Cape Town. Ingrid left her job at the Divisional Council because of a complaint against her that was apparently politically motivated and started working for the publishing firm John Malherbe. It was in this capacity that she helped André prepare the final proofs of his novel *Orgie* [Orgy] in January 1965, still under the impression that they might have a future together. In the middle of February she wrote him a letter in which she expressed her love and told him that she might be pregnant. She also confronted him with the choice between her and his wife.[141] The letter was never posted. Janet Malcolm comments in her 'biography' of Sylvia Plath's biographers, *The silent woman*, that the unsent letter constitutes a genre of its own. By not tearing up the letter and saving it, she writes, 'we are, in fact, saying that our idea is too precious to be entrusted to the gaze of the actual addressee, who may not grasp its worth, so we "send" it to his equivalent in fantasy, on whom we can absolutely count for an understanding and appreciative reading.'[142]

The publication of *Orgie* on 26 March 1965 was to signal the end of André's relationship with Ingrid. The novel was inspired by the triangular relationship between Ingrid, Jack and André. According to Brink's own admission, about a third of the work consists of letters that Ingrid wrote to him.[143] The novel is dedicated to 'Kokon' [Cocoon], his pet name for her, which she also used to sign her letters to him. It tells of a meeting between a man and a woman (referred to only as *he* and *she*). The man is a writer and lecturer, unhappily married to *a*. The woman, who was raised by her grandmother, is rejected by her father and has a love affair with an older man (referred to as *x*). He forces her to have an abortion when she becomes pregnant with their child and then leaves her for another woman. The man and woman meet when he saves her life after she has tried to commit suicide. These events are narrated as flashbacks, because the novel starts with the two both present at a masked ball a year after their first meeting. Their conversation leads nowhere: the woman wants to have a child with the man, while he is unable to commit himself because of his marriage. At the ball the woman is constantly searching for *x*, who has returned to the city. She finally dances away into the night with a stranger, and when the man finds her the next morning he strangles her and kills her in a last passionate embrace. In the spirit of the sixties the novel experiments with narrative techniques, making use of stream of consciousness narration and certain typographical innovations (two narratives running concurrently on one page, horizontal rather than vertical placement of text on the page, black-printed and blank pages, etc.). Though it was scheduled for publication with APB, Bartho Smit was forced to cancel the project because of political intervention and the publisher John Malherbe took it over.[144]

Because of its strongly autobiographical content, some commentators have been tempted to use elements from the novel to reconstruct Ingrid's life. As I have stressed, this is a dangerous move because it disregards the complex interplay between fiction and (auto)biographical fact that comes into play in any literary text. Although Ingrid helped André with the final proofs of the novel, her response to the text seems to have been ambiguous. Her friend Jean du Preez remembered that Ingrid was very excited and enthusiastic about the manuscript, displaying an almost exhibitionistic pleasure in its content.[145] Her sister Anna, on the other hand, recalled Ingrid as saying that André had exposed her with *Orgie*. When Anna asked her why she had allowed him to do so, she said that she felt she should not stand in the way of his art.[146]

Although André continued to see Ingrid in early April, the publication of *Orgie* marked – at least for him – the end of their affair. Years later he wrote to his student Johan van Wyk: 'In a way the publication of *Orgie* really completed the affair: "our" book was now public … "Our" life could not really continue after that' [my translation].[147] At the end of April he wrote to Ingrid and broke off the relationship because he had met another woman, Salomi Louw. According to his memoir, he was under the impression that Ingrid had a new lover with whom she was very happy. Ingrid received the letter on 28 April and phoned André a day later to confront him.[148] The full extent of her feelings becomes clear in

Ingrid Jonker with her daughter Simone, photographed for Ster *magazine. (Courtesy of the Ingrid Jonker Trust)*

another unposted letter, written to her friend Bonnie. She referred to André's 'cruel' letter, saying she was completely dumbfounded after receiving it: 'here, nié na die bloedbad van Spanje nie, nié na *Orgie* nie, nié na al die jare van wag nié, nié nadat ek Jack vir altyd verloor het nie!' [lord, *not* after the bloodbath of Spain, *not* after

Orgie, not after all the years of waiting, *not* after I had lost Jack forever!][149] Ingrid heard the news that André was finally going to divorce his wife and marry Salomi Louw around 19 May, the day she was being interviewed and photographed for an article in the magazine *Ster.* These photographs reveal something of her mood on the day: she looks utterly dejected, listless to the point of lethargy. Only in one of the photographs does her daughter – also in the picture – manage to make her smile. The image speaks volumes about the poignancy of Simone's position during this time. She was taking on the responsibility of being her mother's caretaker, of trying to make her happy, of getting her to act sociably towards the photographers, just as she would try to stop her from committing suicide on the night of her death.

Other relationships
While Ingrid's affair with André was coming to its end, there were other men in her life. She and Jack still saw each other sporadically, as the entries in his diary and her letters to Bonnie show. The fact that he was the one who took her to hospital when she had the anxiety attack early in January 1965 shows that she was still partly dependent on Jack for practical and emotional support. In early February he wrote to her while on his way to the family farm in Natal and encouraged her to start new writing projects: 'It does not matter how – you must write or you are lost. You have the gift. Beside that – alles is ydelheid [all

117

is vanity],' he urged.[150] Even though Ingrid was under the impression that her relationship with André had a future, her letters to Bonnie suggest that Jack still occupied her mind. She referred, for instance, to the emptiness left by the fact that she did not see him often: 'hoe lééf 'n mens met so 'n groot Kimberleyse gat in jou hart?' [how does one líve with such a Big Kimberley Hole in your heart?], she asked at one point.

Despite this, Jack's diary indicates that they saw each other from time to time. More than once he noted that Ingrid pressured him about marriage and threatened suicide, even though he was seeing other women. Ingrid's letters to Bonnie suggest that her feelings towards Jack fluctuated between anger, resentment and love. In March she wrote to Bonnie that she was not seeing 'die grote god Jack' [the great god Jack] any more, implying that she experienced him as distant and condescending. In May, after it became clear that the relationship with André was over, she again turned to Jack for love and reassurance. In a letter written to him while he was in Johannesburg, she expressed her love: 'Be good, take heart, love me with this same indestructable *knowledge* with which I love you, no matter what, look after yourself, come back soon, and write IMMEDIATELY!'[151] In June she wrote to Bonnie, referring to Jack as that '"hero of the campus" JC', whom she didn't see any longer because she could no longer bear his 'emosionele bullebakkery' [emotional bullying]. In spite of this it is clear that Jack remained the one to whom she appealed in moments of distress and despair. It was to him that she would address two suicide notes, trying to explain herself. His diary entry on 9 July 1965, ten days before her death, referred to Ingrid and Bonnie visiting Sea Girt: 'Ingrid is angry & depressed & fierce. I love her & this moment of wildness & passion & despair is a bitter thing. Never have two people been so much at odds, so crossed & contrary.' Despite this, several people who knew them, among them Ingrid's close friend Freda Linde,[152] felt that Jack's coldness lay behind her seeking refuge in sexual relationships with other men. Jack was yet another father figure whose acceptance and approval she sought desperately and without success.

Apart from fleeting relationships with other men like Nico Verboom, there was another person to whom Ingrid became close in the few months before her death. He was the Flemish art student Herman van Nazareth, whom she met on 7 February 1965. In a letter to Bonnie dated 22 March she mentioned that she was 'jazzing around' with artists and a young fellow aged 23 who wanted to marry her (Van Nazareth was actually 28 at the time, three years younger than Ingrid). In May she again wrote to Bonnie, saying that she often went out with him, calling him 'my vriendjie' [my little friend]. According to Van Nazareth they lived together and wanted to get married, but as a poverty-stricken student on a very limited budget he did not have enough money to support them. Van Nazareth became the target of childish displays of jealousy by Jack, whose diary reflected his dislike of Ingrid's new lover. At the beginning of July, Van Nazareth left Cape Town by train on a tour of South Africa.

Work, money, public life, an accident

During the last months of her life Ingrid worked in a succession of jobs. Though she had no great enthusiasm for any of them, she had to provide for herself. She was in dire financial straits and in letters of the time she often declared she was 'broke'. After she left the Divisional Council, she first worked for the publishing firm John Malherbe and then for Citadel Press, reading proofs. She finally quit this job in April because she could no longer tolerate the noise of the printing presses and the boredom of working in this 'Grys Gat' [Grey Hole], as she called it.[153] Among her ideas for earning an income before looking for another job was selling subscriptions to *Contrast*. By June she was working as translator of technical advertisements for Nasionale Tydskrifte, with the prospect of starting as a translator at *Die Burger* on 1 July. She delayed taking up this job until 19 July, after breaking her leg in May. When the cast was taken off late in June, her leg had to be reset because it had not healed properly. The second cast would only be taken off a week before her death. There is more than one story of how her leg was broken: her sister Anna said that it was the result of a scuffle when police broke up a political protest meeting. Herman van Nazareth recalled that her leg was broken in a tussle with waiters who tried to keep them out of the Waldorf Café because he was not wearing a tie. Other sources said that she was in a motorcar accident.[154] Ingrid's diary entry on 24 May only says: 'Afbeen.'[155] Cope wrote in his diary that he confronted Ingrid about the story of the motorcar accident because he felt she was lying and that she then admitted it was broken in a scuffle when she was in the company of Van Nazareth.[156] It was not easy for her to cope with the fracture, not only because it inhibited mobility but also because it made her feel ugly.[157]

Although she was preoccupied with personal problems, Ingrid was not completely cut off from public life in the months before her death. On 26 April she attended a meeting in the Cape Town Drill Hall organised by the Black Sash to protest against a government proclamation prohibiting mixed audiences from attending public events or performances. A photograph in the *Cape Times* shows her listening to the speeches by several speakers, including Uys Krige. She also reacted to the controversy that erupted about a series of hostile articles on the Sestigers in the magazine *Ster*. An editorial accompanying the first of these articles, which featured Breyten Breytenbach, condemned his statement that he was ashamed of being an Afrikaner. This happened after his wife was refused a visa to attend the APB prize-giving ceremony in South Africa because she was Vietnamese and their marriage was illegal under apartheid laws. The editor also challenged other Sestigers either to endorse or repudiate Breyten's statement. Ingrid responded in a letter to the *Sunday Times* in which she called *Ster*'s editorial about Breytenbach libellous. She said she could neither endorse nor repudiate Breytenbach's statement, adding: 'I am not a racialist. I am not anti-German, anti-Jew, anti-English, anti-African, anti-Afrikaner. The lack of integrity and justice shown by certain members of the Afrikaner nation fills me with grief and a sense of loss. Yet the nation has produced fine people as well, of whom I am proud.'[158] She went on to criticise Breytenbach for accepting the prize and then upbraiding his people for not giving his wife a visa, but also defended him against *Ster*'s criticism, saying that it was 'unfair' and 'gross' to say that Afrikaners were ashamed of him. In a private letter to Bonnie, written earlier, she also expressed the opinion that Breyten should first have applied for the visa and then turned down the prize after the visa was refused. Her view seems to have been based on the argument that nothing had been said about the fact that coloureds were being subjected to the same humiliations almost daily (Adam Small would raise the same argument eight years later when Breytenbach was allowed to visit South Africa with his Vietnamese wife, amid great media hype). Ingrid herself was interviewed for this series of articles in *Ster* in May and might have wondered how they were going to represent her. In solidarity with the other Sestigers, she threatened to withdraw permission for the interview to be published. A day before her death, the *Sunday Times* also carried a report on the reaction of Cape writers to the witch-hunt aimed at the Sestigers, in which Ingrid was quoted extensively. She referred to the 'alarm and despondency' caused by the attempts to intimidate and victimise thinking people in all professions and concluded by stating, as she had done before, that writers would not 'come to terms with the enemy'.[159]

Many of Ingrid's friends later remembered that in the last weeks before her death her dejection and desperation were palpable. She was penniless, often hungry, under threat of losing her flat, worried about Simone and not certain if she would be able to write again. Uys gave her some secretarial work because he realised she had no money. To Bonnie, Ingrid wrote that she would not be able to feed her when she came to visit in July and she would be sure to lose weight during her stay. She herself had lost a lot of weight, she wrote, and could no longer be described as '126 lb of poetry', as Herman van Nazareth had done when he first met her in February 1965. Ina, wife of Bill de Klerk, saw Ingrid at a party three weeks before her death; she arrived on foot with Simone after Jack failed to fetch her as he had promised.[160] At the party she spoke of her bitterness about Jack and André to more than one person.

Ingrid's cries of help to those around her were met either with incomprehension or indifference. Her sister Anna remembered that Ingrid phoned her father shortly before her death to ask him whether they could go on a holiday together. Apparently his response was that he would buy her a one-way ticket to Valkenburg. Upon this she suddenly disappeared, until Jack found her in the hospital.[161] On 13 July Ingrid attended a séance,[162] organised by her friend Freda Linde, with Bonnie and a group of others. According to Freda, Ingrid had high expectations of the event because she wanted to communicate with her mother, but the meeting dissolved in laughter when it became clear that the medium was a fake. On this occasion Ingrid mentioned that she needed money and wanted to sell the gold medal she had received as part of the APB prize. After first planning to get Jack to buy the APB prize volume, which was a replica of her book *Rook en oker* with a solid gold plaque inside, and keep it for her until she could buy it back, she suddenly decided to give it to him on 14 July. The dedication to Jack on the title page was dated 10 July 1965 and quoted lines from Walt Whitman's poem 'Good-bye my fancy'.[163] With the privilege of hindsight the message seems clear.

Long indeed have we lived, slept,
    filter'd, become really blended into one
If we go anywhere we'll go together
    to meet what happens
Maybe we'll be better off and blither,
    And learn something

Maybe it is yourself now really
    ushering me into true songs
Maybe it is you the mortal knob really
    undoing, turning
And so finally
Goodbye, my love

The suicide: 'the sum total of my desperation'

The last weeks of Ingrid's life seem to have been ruled
by contradictory impulses. On the one hand she was
still trying to make plans to leave Cape Town and start a
new life in Johannesburg. She even considered applying
for a bursary to study in Belgium.[164] She also continued
her attempts to find money to provide for herself and
Simone. On the other hand there were numerous
indications that she was determined to end her own life.
Stories abound of attempts at suicide at this time, as well
as stories of references to suicide. As far back as February
Jack's diary mentions a newspaper report he read while
in Natal about a young woman who was helped back into
her flat in Three Anchor Bay by an unknown youth after
hanging suspended from the window. 'No names. But I
have a dread all day that this might have been Ingrid,' he
wrote. Her cousin Andries Cilliers reported that he had
had to stop her from jumping from the balcony in her
flat about a month before her death. After her death her
friends discovered that several of them had stories to tell
about trying to stop Ingrid from committing suicide, but

they had never compared notes because of an odd kind of reticence.[165]

That the idea of suicide was foremost in Ingrid's mind for at least some time before the event is clear from the suicide note that she addressed to Jack on 28 June but didn't send to him. In it she declared: 'I can no longer go on living like this, and by the time this reaches you, it will be no good to search for me. I am not threatening you, this is the sum total of my desperation.'[166] In the note she made arrangements that Simone should be sent to her father and assured Jack of her love ('I love you with a desperate love, despite everything that I have done to you'). Looking over her life, she concluded that her most important contributions were her daughter and the volume *Rook en oker*. Her diary entry for the last few days of her life read: 'Stilte' [Silence].

On Friday 16 July she wrote to Bartho Smit to ask him to try and sell the copyright to *Rook en oker* because she needed money desperately. On the same day she also completed the short story ''n Daad van geloof', based on her childhood days with her grandmother and infused with a gentle nostalgia for her grandmother's faith and her own beginnings as a writer. On 17 July she visited Anna and asked her whether Simone could come and stay with her.[167] Her friend Bonnie arrived to visit her for the weekend at her flat in Bonne Esperance in Three Anchor Bay and got the impression that Ingrid was at the end of her tether. Although she seemed excited about taking up the position as translator at *Die Burger*, her friends Lena Oelofse and Marie Prinsloo had misgivings about her state of mind when they saw her for lunch at Uys Krige's in Clifton on Sunday 18 July. Another, less coherent suicide note addressed to Jack and scribbled in a copy of the July edition of *Contrast* shows that they had reason to be worried. 'I am not dying, I hope, to *revenge*, only because my love has failed [...] my darling it is not *your* fault but the fault of my own unworthy make-up. Please look after Simone,' she wrote.[168] On Sunday afternoon she phoned her friend Juliana Bouws because she was feeling so wretched and they had tea before Juliana dropped her off at her psychiatrist.[169] Jack visited her in her flat on the evening of 18 July on his way to attend a function at the American Consulate; they had an argument about her plans for going to Johannesburg which hugely upset her. Bonnie recalled that he tormented her by pretending not to understand when she tried to explain herself.[170]

In the hours that followed, Bonnie and Simone did everything they could to prevent Ingrid from taking her own life. After eleven that night Bonnie and Ingrid went to a restaurant in Sea Point where they drank coffee and chatted to people because Ingrid was feeling so restless. After their return to the flat, Ingrid went out again. Bonnie followed her and tried to persuade her not to commit suicide, but Ingrid was determined. At this point Bonnie realised that she would have to guard Ingrid until morning when she would be able to get help. They walked beside the sea before they went back to the flat, with Ingrid again announcing her intention to end her life that night. After dozing off, Bonnie was woken by Simone, who told her that her mother was lying on the floor by the front door. They heard Ingrid open the door and followed her. Eventually they saw her enter the police station. At that point, Bonnie decided to take Simone, who was very upset, to Jack and Uys in Clifton. When she arrived there they phoned the police in Sea Point, who told them that Ingrid was at the station. Feeling reassured, Bonnie then returned to the flat with Simone. After she put the child to sleep, Bonnie went to the police station to find Ingrid. But when the police informed her that they had already taken Ingrid back to her flat, Bonnie realised she had succeeded in evading them and began searching for her, avoiding the beach, which she subconsciously knew might provide her with an answer. The last person to see Ingrid alive was probably the journalist Terry Herbst. Ingrid stopped him along the Sea Point beachfront in a distraught state and asked him to talk to her, finally leaving him with the words 'Nobody can help me any more'. When Bonnie returned to the police station early in the morning, she was told that Ingrid's body had been found on the beach. Rumours that she had consumed a lot of alcohol and even drugs before committing suicide were refuted by the autopsy, which showed that the cause of death was drowning.

The news of her death drew feelings of shock, dismay and self-reproach. Jack and Uys were asked to identify her body. They were both distraught, especially Jack, as his diary entry for 19 July shows: 'Darling I failed you. There is only one irreparable fault – to lack faith, to lose courage, to be smaller than one's love – I love you a million times.' André, who was in Pretoria at the time, was given the news by a friend before he could hear it on the radio and went blind for several hours on hearing of her death. Ingrid's father was in the Eastern Cape when he heard the news. Rumour had it that he responded coldly when told that she had drowned, asking why they had not pushed her back into the sea.[171] His son Koos denied this strongly, saying that he was with his father at the time and that his only response was that they had to leave for Cape Town immediately. Ingrid's niece Catherine remembered that her mother Anna couldn't stop screaming when she heard of Ingrid's death.[172] Simone was put on an aeroplane to be with her father Piet and his wife Topsi in Johannesburg and was only told what had happened when she arrived there. Because the media descended on the Venters' house, Simone was sent to stay with Topsi's sister on their farm near Philippolis.[173]

The events surrounding the funeral, which took place in Cape Town's Maitland Cemetery on Thursday 22 July, were a sad reflection of the tensions and divisions that marked Ingrid's life. Her friends organised a non-religious ceremony, with a simple wooden coffin, at which a number

129

of her poems were to be read. But Abraham Jonker was offended that Ingrid's friends had taken it upon themselves to organise the funeral and made new arrangements. According to the newspapers, he feared the funeral would be turned into a political event. There would be no church service but a Dutch Reformed minister, the Rev. J.L. van Rooyen, was asked to officiate at the graveside. A more expensive coffin was ordered and it was decided that the pallbearers would be Abraham Jonker, his 23-year-old son Koos and two of Koos's university friends. (In the end the bills for the funeral were sent to Ingrid's friends, who had to pay for everything.) At the graveside the mourners were divided into two groups. On the one side stood the Jonker family (Anna did not attend, in protest against the change in funeral arrangements), their friends and members of the Special Branch. On the other side were her friends, including banned people like Gillian Jewell and Albie Sachs, who had to get special permission to attend. According to Marjorie Wallace, Lulu Jonker came to warn her that those under banning orders would be arrested if any of Ingrid's poems were read, because this would turn the funeral into a political meeting. Jack was so distraught that he sobbed uncontrollably and had to be held back by friends from lunging towards the coffin when it was lowered into the grave. After the Jonker family left, Ingrid's friends approached to throw flowers in the grave. Jack's contribution was a wreath of wild olive which he picked on the slopes above Clifton. André decided not to attend the funeral because he felt his presence could turn what should be a private event into a public spectacle. Herman van Nazareth, who arrived back in Cape Town on 20 July only to be told the news of Ingrid's death, was appalled by what happened at the graveside, referring to the event as a badly performed comedy.

At the graveside Jan Rabie proposed that they all meet again on Sunday 25 July to give Ingrid a proper funeral, one at which they could read her poetry and mourn her in an appropriate manner. At this second funeral, attended by more than a hundred of her friends, Uys spoke about Ingrid's poetry and Jan read some of her poems, after which those present were invited to say something in honour of Ingrid. This time Ingrid's sister Anna attended. In an incident that shows how much Ingrid and her friends were still regarded with hostility and suspicion, a high-school teacher, Jan le Roux from Riviersonderend, was prevented from taking his pupils, who loved Ingrid's poems, to the funeral by the local dominee and the school principal. True to their religious upbringing, these pupils held their own prayer meeting for Ingrid instead, where they read a few of her poems.[174]

At the second funeral Jan Rabie announced that an Ingrid Jonker Prize would be instituted for debut poets and asked for contributions to the prize money from those present. The sculptor Bill Nash promised to design and make the medal. The Ingrid Jonker Prize is still awarded annually to a debut poet in either Afrikaans or English and is judged by writers, not literary critics or academics. Ingrid's memory was also honoured by the publication in 1966 of a collection of essays, *In memoriam Ingrid Jonker*, edited by Jan. The most important contributions were by Jack and Uys, but there were also pieces by literary academics and a variety of Afrikaans, English and Dutch poems written in her honour by friends like Barend J. Toerien, Freda Linde, Ruth Miller, Richard Rive, David Lytton, Cees de Jong and Jack himself. This book has become a collector's item because it was withdrawn shortly after publication when it came to light that the poem attributed to Simon Vinkenoog was actually written by the Flemish poet Paul van Ostaijen for the German-Jewish poet Else Lasker-Schüler.

Responses to Ingrid's suicide

Ingrid Jonker's death affected those close to her very deeply. The oft-quoted words from Arthur Miller's play *After the fall*, 'A suicide kills two people, Maggie, that's what it's for', seem especially appropriate in the case of Ingrid's father. After her suicide Abraham Jonker's health went into rapid decline. Apparently he drank heavily until his death of an aneurism on 10 January 1966, a little less than six months after his daughter's death.[175] According to his daughter Suzanne, he seemed to be a broken man after Ingrid's suicide.[176] Jack was overcome by feelings of guilt and remorse. In a letter to Uys Krige on 5 August 1965, he wrote: 'Everything was a betrayal and mine above all, not thrice ere the crowing cock, but with every hour of the night, how can I have betrayed the one woman I loved & love to the last breath? How does one do this? God knows it is the ultimate bitterness and agony.'[177] In André Brink's case, the news of her death was followed by a long period of disorientation and aimlessness in his creative work.

Although Ingrid's daughter Simone was only seven years old and probably could not fully comprehend what happened, she suffered greatly from the loss of her mother. When interviewed in an early documentary about Ingrid's life she acknowledged the psychological damage caused by her mother's suicide, but also said that she accepted her mother's choice. 'She wanted to die. It was something she had thought about very deeply. It was her choice.'[178] Living with her mother through the final months of her life seems to have given her insight into the plight of someone who could not face life any more. The American literary critic Norman Holland has argued that even though it is tempting to invest literary suicide with symbolic or transcendental meaning, as Al Alvarez did in his book *The savage god*, we must also acknowledge the suicidal person's agency, her responsibility and her right to act. 'Perhaps we can change our style and accept the fact that suicide, even literary suicide, for all that we can invest in it of the sacred, is still a human act. It embodies a choice among alternatives made through the same principles of human motivation as other choices, even though this is a choice to end choice itself,' he wrote in an essay on literary suicide.[179] This comment brings yet another perspective to our understanding of Ingrid Jonker's suicide. Her death has been interpreted in many different ways: as a response to the call of the unconscious symbolised by the sea, a return to the womb of the mother she lost as a child, the inevitable outcome of her unhappy childhood, a turning to the sea as the only lover that would accept her unconditionally, a destiny she was driven to by an unfeeling father and a harsh political system. Perhaps the most imaginative and sometimes the most insightful readings of her suicide have been given by fellow writers in poems that celebrate her life and speculate on the reasons for her death.

Many saw in Ingrid's death an indictment of apartheid society. Her suicide was attributed to her intense discomfort with South Africa's racial politics, the narrow-mindedness of the country's censorship laws, the bigotry of petty apartheid and the unfeeling manner of many white people in South Africa towards people of colour. This interpretation was reinforced by the coincidence of her suicide with that of the black journalist Nat Nakasa, who had been editor of the literary magazine *The Classic*. When he was awarded the Niemann scholarship to study in the United States in 1965, his application for a passport was denied by the government. He was forced to leave South Africa on a one-way exit permit and to abandon his editorship of *The Classic*.[180] He committed suicide by jumping off a building in New York on 14 July 1965, his death coming just five days before that of Ingrid. Though their situations were completely different, the near simultaneous deaths of these two young writers moved a number of writers. Both Wilma Stockenström and William Plomer wrote poems to commemorate and mourn Nakasa's and Jonker's end. Richard Rive wrote: 'Ingrid and Nat died continents apart. She was experiencing a different kind of exile right inside South Africa. Their causes of death were the same: their inability to adapt, and the inability of others to cater for their insight and sensitivity.'[181] Athol Fugard honoured both in a piece published in *The Classic* in 1966 in which he commented with bitterness: 'We have paid again. Let us make no mistake; this was another instalment in the terrible price and South Africa – that profligate spender of human lives – paid it.'[182] In his response to her death Laurens van der Post also placed Ingrid's personal life within the larger frame of South Africa's political life: 'Her suicide to me is almost like the suicide of Afrikanerdom. She was rejected by her father, her people, and her lover, even Uys, so self-absorbed in his own emotions,' he wrote in a letter to William Plomer.[183]

Ingrid's death was also seen as a leave-taking of Afrikaans literature, especially as the literary and political establishment of the time conceived it. At the time of her death Ingrid was part of the Sestigers' rebellion against censorship and apartheid politics in general. Jan Rabie was the first to ask what kind of society it was that cast out its rebellious young writers and cosseted the tame ones. His contribution to the volume *In memoriam Ingrid Jonker* was an angry reflection on the fact that Afrikaans literature had lost four of its most important young poets in the early 1960s: Ingrid Jonker and Barnard Gilliland to death, Breyten Breytenbach and Peter Blum because of political discontent. Years later, Breyten Breytenbach would also write a poem on this subject while serving time as a political prisoner. In his 'Ballade van ontroue bemindes' [Ballad of unfaithful lovers], based on François Villon's 'Ballade des dames du temps jadis', he referred to Ingrid Jonker, Peter Blum and himself as unfaithful lovers who had betrayed Afrikaans poetry by taking leave in one way or another. Wondering what his own end as a poet would be, he concluded with the poignant lines 'Kyk wat het geword van Pieter Blum. / Kyk waar lê I. witgraat in die donker' [See what happened to Pieter Blum. / See where I. lies white-boned in the dark]. For most, her untimely death constituted a significant loss for Afrikaans literature and prevented her from achieving great things as a poet and writer.

Ingrid's death is often compared with other literary suicides, those of the American poets Sylvia Plath and Anne Sexton as well as Virginia Woolf. On the surface the similarities, especially with Plath, are indeed striking.

Sylvia Plath committed suicide at the age of 30 in 1963; Ingrid Jonker was 31 when she died in 1965. They both lost one parent at an early age and had a complex relationship with the other. They both battled depression and received psychiatric treatment. They were both deserted by the men in their lives shortly before their deaths and were both the mothers of young children when they died. They both left behind relatively small oeuvres and their literary estates became the subject of complicated dealings after their deaths. More importantly, both Ingrid Jonker and Sylvia Plath extended the horizon of expectations for women's writing within their own literary traditions. This common feature has been extensively pursued in Afrikaans literary studies.

In conclusion, Ingrid Jonker's suicide still moves people, arouses their pity and fear, because it was located at a point where events in her personal life intersected with great turning points in South African history. In her personal biography, what stands out is the emotional devastation caused by her unsuccessful relationships with Jack and André, which in turn evoked the spectre of her 'verstote kindertyd' [outcast childhood],[184] the problematic relationship with her father, the struggle to provide for herself and her daughter, the difficulty to regain enough self-confidence after breaking her leg and her doubts as to whether she would be able to write again. At the same time her general outlook on life was strongly marked by the political events of the early 1960s. The pervasive atmosphere of repression and emergency could not but affect her personal being, not least because it impacted so negatively on her relationship with her father.

7

Afterlife

'And above all do not make me a thing'
– Ingrid Jonker after Louis MacNeice, 'Prayer
before birth'

Literary estate

On 30 July 1965 Jack wrote in his diary that Ingrid had
made a will in which she appointed him her executor.
Although this will was invalid because there were no
witnesses, Jack was eventually appointed executor of her
estate and proceeded to set up the Ingrid Jonker Trust, for
which he and her sister Anna acted as trustees, to protect
Simone's copyright interests in her mother's work.[185]
Her movable possessions were bought from the estate
by Anna, and Jack acquired the copyright to her work on
behalf of Simone. His diary indicates that he spent the
months after Ingrid's death collecting all her documents,
papers, letters and diaries, some of which were used by
the police in the investigation into her death. He also
tried to find all existing photographs of her and sorted
her remaining poems so that they could be published.

As early as September 1965 he expressed the intention to donate all Ingrid's papers and manuscripts to the South African Public Library. Twelve years after her death he placed her papers, including various manuscript versions of her poems, her diaries and a number of letters, in the care of the National English Literary Museum in Grahamstown.[186] The papers were catalogued and placed in a restricted area but could be consulted for research. Johan van Wyk used the documents in the mid-1980s while doing research for his doctoral thesis under the supervision of André Brink, then professor in the Department of Afrikaans at Rhodes University. Two years before his death in 1991, Jack gave permission for Ingrid's papers to be returned to Anna because she intended to write a biography about Ingrid. After the material was returned to her, Anna alleged that pages from her sister's Paris diary had been torn out, that some of Brink's letters to Ingrid had been removed and that letters from Laurens van der Post were torn up while the papers were in the safe-keeping of the museum, implicating Brink among others. Both the museum director, Malcolm Hacksley, and Brink vehemently denied these claims, the former referring to a report in which Anna admitted that she had torn up some of Brink's most intimate letters to Ingrid because she regarded them as pornographic and valueless for research, while Brink threatened Anna with a law-suit if she persisted with her accusations.[187] Three years after Anna's death in 1997 the papers were sold to the Dutch poet Gerrit Komrij by her son Anthony Bairos for the sum of R50,000. Ingrid's daughter Simone tried to institute legal proceedings to stop the sale of the documents, which she felt belonged to her, but she was unsuccessful.[188] The papers were with Komrij until his recent death in mid-2012. Although he had intimated that they might be placed with the Dutch Literary Museum in The Hague or the South African Institute in Amsterdam, the documents are still inaccessible and it remains uncertain what their fate will be.

Posthumous publications: *Kantelson*, translations, anthologies, collected writings

The volume *Windroos*, which was accepted for publication by APB's Bartho Smit at the end of 1964, was finally published in February 1966 under the title *Kantelson* [Tilting/Tilted sun]. Jack Cope conducted the final negotiations with Smit and prepared the collection for publication. It contained the poems written after Ingrid met Brink in March 1963 and reflected the major events in the last two years of her life. It also included her last three poems, written after Bartho Smit had received the manuscript from her.[189]

Although the volume is close to *Rook en oker* in its style and execution, it lacks its impact and coherence. Love is still an important thematic preoccupation, although most of the poems reflect a consciousness that love is double-faced and treacherous. The poem 'Tokolos'

[Tokoloshe], for instance, evokes a sphere of innocence with children playing in the wood, although there is already the knowledge that love is a tokoloshe who has a light- as well as a dark-sided face. There are, however, also moments of serene certainty about the integrity of love in 'Gesig van die liefde' [The face of love] as well as moments of playful sexual innuendo, as in 'Twee harte' [Two hearts]. Most of the love poems reflect a consciousness of treachery ('Daar is net een vir altyd'), of the need to forget ('O die halfmaan'), of unrequited waiting ('Wagtyd in Amsterdam') and betrayal ('Alles wat breek'). The image of the mirror, so prominent in *Rook en oker*, resurfaces in these poems. Here the image points to the poet's desperate need to mirror herself in the beloved other, to reassure herself of her own existence by being reflected in someone else's love. In the poem 'As jy weer skryf' [When you write again] she writes: 'ek het jou saamgedra soos 'n spieël' [I carried you with me like a mirror]. In 'Waterval van mos en son' [Waterfall of moss and sun] she finds her own face in that of the beloved. What is new in this volume is the shading of melancholy into bitterness and disillusionment in poems such as 'Met hulle is ek' and 'Ek dryf in die wind', in which the speaking subject expresses her conviction that society has become corrupt.

After her death, it was not long before Ingrid's poems began to be included in anthologies of Afrikaans poetry as well as of South African poetry in translation.

Eight of her poems were included in *The Penguin book of South African verse*, edited by Jack and Uys in 1968. Negotiations to have her poems included in the most important Afrikaans anthology of the time, D.J. Opperman's influential *Groot verseboek*, were already under way at the time of her death. The 1967 impression of the second edition used six of her poems, among which was 'Die kind.' Since then her work has become a staple in Afrikaans anthologies as well as anthologies of South African poetry such as Denis Hirson's *The lava of the land* (1997) and Michael Chapman's *The new century of South African poetry* (2002). It is also routinely included in anthologies of women's writing from South Africa.

A selection of her poems translated into English was first published in 1968 under the title *Selected poems* by Jonathan Cape in London. Work on the translation of these poems had started in 1960 with the help of Ingrid herself, but the final product was a joint effort by Jack Cope and William Plomer. A new selection of her verse entitled *Black butterflies*, translated by André Brink and Antjie Krog with the help of Ingrid de Kok, was published in 2007 by Human & Rousseau. Her poems have also been translated into a wide variety of languages, including Zulu, Hindi, Dutch, German, Russian and Polish.

The first edition of Ingrid's collected writings, her *Versamelde werke*, was edited by Jack Cope and published in 1975 by Perskor, the publishing conglomerate that took over APB in 1971.[190] It included her poetry, the

143

play *'n Seun na my hart,* five short stories as well as two autobiographical pieces and the transcript of an interview with the SABC. Abraham de Vries was later contracted by Perskor to compile and edit a second, revised edition of Ingrid's *Versamelde werke,* which eventually appeared in 1983. After Mandela quoted Ingrid in parliament in 1994, the Cape Town publisher Human & Rousseau acquired the rights to publish a new edition of her *Versamelde werke.* This time it was edited by Anna, who made use of Ingrid's surviving documents in her possession at the time. Such was the demand for Ingrid's poetry that this third edition of her collected works was available before 1994 was out.

The making of an icon: the Afrikaner dissident, Marilyn Monroe, literary inspiration

In the years after her death Ingrid Jonker grew into a many-sided icon. Depending on the vantage point, she has been described as an Afrikaner dissident, a South African Marilyn Monroe or a literary inspiration.

As already indicated, several people expressed the conviction that the despair leading to Ingrid's death could be, at least partly, related to her disillusionment with South Africa's oppressive racial politics and the increasing clampdown on freedom of speech. Whether one agrees with this view or not, there is no denying the strength and persistence of this perception. The journalist Johann Potgieter wrote in 1982 that Ingrid Jonker's death was a pivotal event in the history of the Sestigers. It made her the greatest symbol of their 'cultural insurrection' and created the image of her as martyr for this 'cultural revolt in the heart of Afrikanerdom'.[191] Although Potgieter may be overstating the case of Ingrid Jonker's martyrdom, he is correct in gauging the symbolic value her death has come to attain in the eyes of many. It has led to her inclusion in the ranks of dissident writers in Afrikaans by commentators like Peter Horn in *Kap der Guten Hoffnung* (1980), J. Alvarez-Pereyre in *Poetry of commitment* (1984), Jack Cope in *The adversary within* (1991) and Dan O'Meara in *Forty lost years* (1996).[192] This image was further reinforced by ANC politicians' references to 'Die kind'. It was especially Mandela's words that she was an 'Afrikaner woman who transcended a particular experience and became a South African, an African and a citizen of the world' that fixed the image of Ingrid Jonker as Afrikaner dissident in the public imaginary. Her iconic status as South African was confirmed by the posthumous award of the Order of Ikhamanga for 'her excellent contribution to literature and a commitment to the struggle for human rights and democracy in South Africa' in 2004. It was further reinforced when she became one of the South Africans commemorated by the *Sunday Times* Heritage Project in a trail of 35 street memorials erected to mark the paper's centenary in 2006.

For many, Ingrid Jonker is also a sexual icon whose appeal lies in the irresistible 'combination of sex,

145

Portrait of Ingrid Jonker. (Courtesy of the National English Literary Museum, Grahamstown)

rebellion and death', as Michael Cope wrote in *Intricacy*. Her physical attractiveness and exuberant sexuality, combined with a distinct vulnerability, have prompted more than one commentator to compare her with

Marilyn Monroe. Although the comparison obscures crucial differences, it is based on both women's inability to find lasting happiness in their relationships with men and their increasing desperation in the months before they took their own lives. For many, Ingrid Jonker's sexual allure is heightened by the image of a bohemian life lived outside the rigid moral boundaries set by society in the sixties and her rebellion against the political principles of Afrikanerdom, even though it meant forgoing the approval of her father, which she so desperately needed.

For Afrikaans writers and readers alike, Ingrid Jonker has also become an important literary icon. Because of the tragic circumstances of her death and the direct appeal of her poetry, she is the one poet that Afrikaans-speaking school-children are most likely to relate to, hers the one name that non-readers of poetry are likely to know. The question whether her work has been overrated because of her tragic life and death has often been raised. Literary critics and academics differ on this point: some commentators like Kannemeyer, Lindenberg and Driesse find that the evaluation of her work has been influenced by the details of her life and that her reputation rests mainly on a few sensitive and well-made poems; whereas others like Johan van Wyk and Joan Hambidge feel that her fame as a poet is fully justified. Even though her oeuvre is small, there is no doubt that she occupies a significant and a singular place among the many strong Afrikaans poets writing at the time. She brought a distinctive voice to the writing of the Sestigers, with whom she shared a break with tradition, assimilation of influences from a wider world literature and a sensitivity to the social and political exigencies of the time. Despite appearing to be deceptively simple, her poems are tightly constructed, dictated by an inner logic that combines a flowing musicality with inventive imagery, accurate word-play and emotional conviction. Although she disliked the artificiality of the distinction between male and female poetry (especially when it was made to belittle the work of women), she acknowledged the fact that she wrote as a woman even when she was given the back-handed compliment that at her best she wrote 'like a man.'[193] Her contribution to expanding the female tradition in Afrikaans poetry should therefore not be underestimated, especially through the candour and perceptiveness she brought to the writing of female experience. The influence of her poetry is best illustrated by the example of Antjie Krog, who published her debut volume in 1970, five years after Ingrid's death, and subsequently developed into one of the major poets in Afrikaans. Ingrid Jonker's candid and unpretentious poetry paved the way for Krog's transgressive themes and the poetic style which Krog herself described as 'kaalvoet' [barefoot].[194]

Ingrid Jonker's status as a literary icon is also affirmed by the wide range of creative responses her poetry has elicited from other South African poets, writing in both English and Afrikaans. Many of these poems focus on the life of the poet as much as on her poetry, as can be seen in the contributions included in the 1966 volume *Ingrid Jonker: In memoriam* as well as in the poems about her that followed after Mandela's reference revived general interest in her. Afrikaans poets had, however, been engaging with her poetry even before then. They acknowledged her influence by re-visiting and re-writing her poems, often commenting on her poetic vision in order to find their own poetical voices. The classic poems from her oeuvre like 'Ontvlugting', 'Bitterbessie dagbreek' and 'Die kind' have inspired imaginative re-writings by Afrikaans poets like Antjie Krog, Johann de Lange, Joan Hambidge, Fanie Olivier, Lina Spies and Daniel Hugo. 'Die kind' has for example been evoked many times, its message recontextualised to comment on a new set of circumstances, whether it be the death of Hector Pieterson in a poem by Fanie Olivier or the possible demise of the Afrikaans language in a poem by Clinton V. du Plessis. The parallels between Ingrid Jonker, Sylvia Plath, Anne Sexton and the Russian poet Marina Tsvetaeva have also been elaborated in poems by Lina Spies, Joan Hambidge and Petra Müller. Moreover, several of Ingrid's poems have been set to music and performed by, among others, Laurika Rauch, Ddisselblom and Chris Chameleon, the last-mentioned achieving great success in capturing the lyricism of her poetry in two collections on compact disc, *Ek herhaal jou* (2005) and *As jy weer skryf* (2011).

No one face

In the end one comes to the realisation that trying to reconstruct Ingrid Jonker's personality is like piecing together a multiplicity of mirror-like shards, gathered from a variety of sources, that reflect and bounce off each other.

There can be little doubt that Ingrid's childhood years had a huge impact on her life. Losing her mother to cancer when she was 11, and being taken away from her beloved grandmother to live with a father she had scarcely seen before, did not give her a secure start in life. A letter she wrote to Laurens van der Post in August 1964 gave an indication of the impact her past had on her: 'I know there are other things in life apart from love, but one has to have a basis to go out from. Without it, my whole wretched past lifts up its dreadful head, and looks at me with that sad and waste look which paralyses me with terror.'[195] This statement is an important key to Ingrid's psychological and emotional make-up: the emotional wounds she suffered in childhood led to an irrevocable belief in the importance of love and a desperate need for recognition and affirmation. These she did not always find in her family either by blood or marriage. Her relationship with her father was compromised by his inability to acknowledge her success as a writer and later by their political differences. There are also indications that the relationship between Ingrid and her older sister Anna was not ideal. Although Anna suggested in interviews that she fulfilled a motherly and

150

protective role in Ingrid's life, several of Ingrid's friends as well as her psychiatrist observed that the relationship was difficult because of Anna's jealousy and her attempts to complicate Ingrid's relationship with their father.[196] Juliana Bouws put it very strongly when she commented that Ingrid was 'weggooigoed' [a cast-off] because her father favoured Anna.[197] Nor did her marriage to Pieter Venter bring her the happiness and fulfilment she sought. On the one hand she desperately wanted marriage and a child; on the other she seemed unwilling or unable to fulfil the conventional role of a wife in a bourgeois marriage. The relationships with Jack Cope and André Brink that followed could also not bring her the happiness she sought. The one person from whom she received unconditional love was her daughter Simone, with whom she was besotted, even as she struggled to cope with the responsibilities of parenthood. The story of Ingrid's relationship with her daughter is not an unfamiliar one. It is the story of a single parent who has to rely on family, friends and a series of nameless servants to help care for her child when she cannot do so herself. It is the story of a mother who desperately loves her child but is distracted by the financial responsibility of caring for her, the emotional upheavals caused by her sexual relationships with men, the traumatic history of her relationship with her own parents, and loyalty to her vocation as a poet.

Although she had no university education, Ingrid was intellectually curious and driven by a passion for literature.

Her reading experience was catholic and she read widely in Afrikaans, English, Dutch, American and Spanish literature. Names like those of Dylan Thomas, Virginia Woolf, Jean-Paul Sartre, Simone de Beauvoir, Sybren Polet, Henry Miller, J.D. Salinger, George Barker and Scott Fitzgerald crop up in her letters and her bookshelves contained works by Shakespeare, John Keats, Herman Hesse, Friedrich Hölderlin and others. Although she often complained about the mind-numbing dullness of her work as proofreader for publishers or as translator for official bodies, she still did the work with precision. Nancy Baines was one of those who spoke of the dedication with which she helped edit volumes of *Contrast*. Friends recalled that she would demand their full attention when she wanted it, whether to listen to her poems or her personal problems, but that she would also selflessly help them when she could. Such was her extraordinary impact on people, her forceful personality, that several of her writer-friends used her as a model for fictional characters in their novels. She served as inspiration for characters in Berta Smit's *Die vrou en die bees* (1964), André Brink's *Orgie* (1965) and several of his other novels, Jack Cope's *The dawn comes twice* (1969), Jan Rabie's *Klipwieg* (1970) and Karel Schoeman's *Die noorderlig* (1975). Some of these fictionalised portraits are remarkably vibrant, capturing the living person in a way that biographical writing rarely can.

As more information becomes available, the picture that we are able to draw of Ingrid Jonker will become more rounded, even though it will never be complete. Even for those closest to her there was something elusive in her personality. Freda Linde used the image of quicksilver which takes on the form of its container, to describe her.[198] Ingrid herself had a horror of fixity. After her death Jack Cope wrote that she disliked being called by her own name and had many nicknames, each expressing in its way an evasion that kept her indefinable.[199] André Brink said in an interview that she never wanted to be captured or summarised and referred to her quoting lines from Louis MacNeice's 'Prayer before birth': 'And above all do not make me a thing, a thing with one face like water held in a hand would spill me, otherwise kill me'.[200]

Ingrid Jonker has no one face. Other faces are waiting to be discovered.

Notes

1   Uys Krige, 'Soos in haarself eindelik die ewigheid haar verander',
    in Jan Rabie (ed.), *In memoriam Ingrid Jonker* (Cape Town,
    1966), p. 51.
2   There were theses written by O.E. Driesse (1971), Erna Sadie
    (1978) and Johan van Wyk (1983) as well as a psychological
    study by L.M. van der Merwe (1978). Also keeping her memory
    alive was a performance of her play (1970), a programme
    featuring her poetry *Jy't my gekierang Dolie* (1970), Afrikaans
    radio programmes devoted to her memory in 1978 and
    1979, Esther Nasser's ballet *Fragments of Jonker* (1983) and
    a commemoration of her fiftieth birthday organised by the
    Afrikaans Writers' Guild.
3   André Brink, *A fork in the road* (Cape Town, 2009), p. 111.
4   Susan Sontag, *On photography* (London, 2008), p. 24.
5   Paul John Eakin (ed.), *The ethics of life writing* (Ithaca &
    London, 2004), p. 8–15.
6   Ina de Klerk (wife of W.A. de Klerk) in L.M. van der Merwe,
    Gesprekke oor Ingrid Jonker (Hermanus, 2006), p.166; J.C. Steyn,
    N.P. van Wyk Louw: 'n Lewensverhaal. Deel 1 (Cape Town, 1998),
    p. 118.
7   Western Cape Archives, CSC 2/1/1/1247: 333.
8   A.C. Cilliers, *Die silwer soom* (Cape Town, 1959), pp. 78–82.
9   Ingrid Jonker, *Versamelde werke* (Johannesburg, 1975), p. 201.
10 Cilliers, *Die silwer soom*, p. 81.

11   Ingrid Jonker, *Versamelde werke* (Johannesburg, 1975), pp.
     201–7.
12   Anna Jonker, 'Want elkeen het sy Gordonsbaai', *Tydskrif vir
     Letterkunde*, 17, 1 (1979), pp. 5–27.
13   A.C. Cilliers, *Lewensavontuur 2* (Cape Town, 1972), p. 73.
14   This quote comes from an autobiographical piece written for
     Die Vaderland. It was included in the first and second editions
     of Ingrid Jonker's collected works, but not the third edition. See
     Ingrid Jonker, *Versamelde werke* (Johannesburg, 1975), p. 204.
15   Anna Jonker, 'Want elkeen het sy Gordonsbaai', p. 10.
16   Western Cape Archives, CSC 2/1/1/1247: 333.
17   Death notice, *Die Burger*, 9 June 1944.
18   All the Afrikaans versions of Ingrid Jonker's poems are quoted
     from the third edition of Ingrid Jonker's collected works; see
     Ingrid Jonker, *Versamelde werke* (Cape Town, 1994). All the
     translated versions of her poems are quoted from Ingrid Jonker,
     Black butterflies: Selected poems. Translated by André Brink and
     Antjie Krog (Cape Town, 2007), except when stated otherwise.
19   Ingrid Jonker, *Versamelde werke* (Johannesburg, 1975), p. 204.
20   According to Anna Jonker, their grandmother lived almost until
     Ingrid got married in 1956; see Van der Merwe, *Gesprekke oor
     Ingrid Jonker*, p. 220. This is borne out by Andries Cilliers, son of
     A.C. Cilliers and cousin of Anna and Ingrid: he remembers that
     she died while he was in Oxford from 1956 to 1957.
21   Anna Jonker in Van der Merwe, *Gesprekke oor Ingrid Jonker*, p.
     22; Petrovna Metelerkamp, *Ingrid Jonker: Beeld van 'n digterslewe*
     (Hermanus, 2003), p. 30.
22   Anna Jonker says they lodged in a room in St Michael's Road,
     Tamboerskloof; see Van der Merwe, *Gesprekke oor Ingrid Jonker*,
     p. 182. Rieta Burgers remembered that they lodged in Madeira
     House, a boarding house in Kloofstreet; see Metelerkamp, *Ingrid
     Jonker*, p. 47.
23   Elretha Louw, 'In my arms digby die Seine …', *Huisgenoot*, 16
     June 1994, p. 19.
24   Laurens van der Post, in the documentary by Helena Nogueira,
     Ingrid Jonker: Her lives and time (2007).
25   Anna Jonker in Van der Merwe, *Gesprekke oor Ingrid Jonker*, pp.
     216–32.
26   André Brink in Van der Merwe, *Gesprekke oor Ingrid Jonker*, p.
     237; Brink, *A fork in the road*, p. 96.

27 Berta Smit in Van der Merwe, *Gesprekke oor Ingrid Jonker*, p. 118.

28 Ina de Klerk (wife of W.A. de Klerk) in Van der Merwe, *Gesprekke oor Ingrid Jonker*, pp. 166–7.

29 Henk van Woerden, 'De dag heeft een smalle schaduw', in Ingrid Jonker, *Ik herhaal je*. Translated by Gerrit Komrij (Amsterdam, 2000), pp. 158–9.

30 'Jonker, Abraham, Hendrik', *Standard encyclopaedia of Southern Africa*, 6 (Cape Town, Nasou), pp. 236–7.

31 W.A. de Klerk in Van der Merwe, *Gesprekke oor Ingrid Jonker*, p. 162.

32 Anna Jonker, in Metelerkamp, *Ingrid Jonker*, p. 48.

33 Ingrid Jonker, *Versamelde werke* (Johannesburg, 1975), pp. 204–5; Metelerkamp, *Ingrid Jonker*, p. 48.

34 Quoted by Johan van Wyk, *Gesig van die liefde* (Durban, 1999), p. 63.

35 L.M. van der Merwe, *Ingrid Jonker: 'n Psigologiese analise* (PhD, University of Pretoria, 1978), pp. 262–3.

36 Ingrid Jonker, *Versamelde werke* (Johannesburg, 1975), pp. 205 & 216.

37 Anna Jonker, in Van der Merwe, *Gesprekke oor Ingrid Jonker*, p. 229.

38 Berta Smit in Van der Merwe, *Gesprekke oor Ingrid Jonker*, p. 117; Huibrecht Steenkamp in Van der Merwe, *Gesprekke oor Ingrid Jonker*, p. 226.

39 Information in Metelerkamp, *Ingrid Jonker*, pp. 62–77; Cor Pama in Van der Merwe, *Gesprekke oor Ingrid Jonker*, pp. 108–11.

40 Van der Merwe, *Ingrid Jonker*, pp. 262–3, lists these poems. The 1994 edition of Jonker's *Versamelde werke* anthologises most of them.

41 Jack Cope in Metelerkamp, *Ingrid Jonker*, p. 86.

42 Interview with Aletta Greyling published in *Die Transvaler* on 6 March 1964, See Ingrid Jonker, *Versamelde werke* (Johannesburg, 1983), p. 214.

43 Dot van der Merwe, '22-jarige dogter van L.V. publiseer bundel', *Die Burger*, 23 June 1956.

44 Berta Smit in Van der Merwe, *Gesprekke oor Ingrid Jonker*, p. 118.

45 J.C. Kannemeyer, *Die goue seun: Die lewe en werk van Uys Krige* (Cape Town, 2002), p. 535; NELM, Cope papers, Jack Cope diary, 28 January 1960.

46 Jan Rabie, *Jan Rabie: Sestigers in woord en beeld* (Johannesburg, 1986), p. 25; Brink, introduction to *Black butterflies*, p. 13; Amanda Botha, *Marjorie Wallace: Drif en vreugde* (Claremont, 2006), p. 77.

47 Uys Krige, 'Soos in haarself eindelik die ewigheid haar verander', p. 52.

48 Ingrid Jonker, *Versamelde werke* (Johannesburg, 1975), p. 235.

49 Peter Clark, in the documentary by Saskia van Schaik, *Korreltjie niks is my dood*, 2001.

50 Richard Rive, *Writing black* (Cape Town, 1981), p. 111.

51 Kannemeyer, *Die goue seun*, p. 563.

52 Kannemeyer, *Die goue seun*, p. 488; Michael Cope, *Intricacy: A meditation on memory* (Cape Town, 2005), p. 202.

53 Kannemeyer, *Die goue seun*, p. 534.

54 Jack Cope, *English in Africa*, 7, 2 (1980), pp. 4–6.

55 NELM, Cope papers, Jack Cope diary, 16 August 1957 and 27 August 1957.

56 Elmari Rautenbach, ''n Olyftak vir onse Ingrid', *De Kat,* July 1994, p. 52.

57 Michael Cope, *Intricacy*, p. 146.

58 Albie Sachs, in Michael Cope, *Intricacy*, p. 23.

59 Albie Sachs, in Michael Cope, *Intricacy*, p. 24.

60 Marjorie Wallace, in Nogueira, *Ingrid Jonker*.

61 Letter to Jean du Preez, in Metelerkamp, *Ingrid Jonker*, p. 104.

62 Breyten Breytenbach in Van Schaik, *Korreltjie niks is my dood*.

63 Berta Smit in Van der Merwe, *Gesprekke oor Ingrid Jonker*, p. 124.

64 Topsi Smit in Nogueira, *Ingrid Jonker*.

65 Letter to Cope in Metelerkamp, *Ingrid Jonker*, p. 103.

66 Metelerkamp, *Ingrid Jonker*, pp. 94 & 97.

67 Letter to Cope, in Metelerkamp, *Ingrid Jonker*, p. 101.

68 Letter to Cope, in Metelerkamp, *Ingrid Jonker*, p. 99.

69 Ingrid Jonker, *Versamelde werke* (Cape Town, 1994), pp. 163–73.

70 Metelerkamp, *Ingrid Jonker*, p. 99.

71 Western Cape Archives, CSC 2/1/1/2134: 254.

72 Piet Muller, in Metelerkamp, *Ingrid Jonker*, p. 113.

73 Metelerkamp, *Ingrid Jonker*, p. 17; NELM, Cope papers, Jack Cope diary, 11 March 1960.

74 David Maposa, 'Little boy's story lives on', *Cape Argus,* 15 February 2008.

75 Piet Müller, in Metelerkamp, *Ingrid Jonker*, p. 110.

76   Brink wrote that she went to the police station in Philippi to see the body of the dead child; see *A fork in the road,* p. 100; Cope wrote in his diary on 7 April 1960 that Ingrid went out to Nyanga to collect publicity photographs of the troops (NELM, Cope papers).

77   Jack Cope, 'The world of *Contrast', English in Africa,* 7, 2 (1980), p. 14.

78   Ingrid Jonker, *Selected poems.* Translated by Jack Cope and William Plomer (Cape Town, 1988), p. 27.

79   Rautenbach, "'n Olyftak vir onse Ingrid', p. 51.

80   NELM, Cope papers, Jack Cope diary, 14 June 1963.

81   Oliver Tambo, Speech at the International Conference on 'Children, repression and the law in apartheid South Africa', 1987, http://www.anc.org.za/show.php?id=4539 [accessed 20 January 2012].

82   Thabo Mbeki, State of the Nation Address 2004, http://www.info.gov.za/speeches/2004/04020610561002.htm; Thabo Mbeki, State of the Nation Address 2006, http://www.info.gov.za/speeches/2006/06020310531001.htm [accessed 20 January 2012].

83   This story was included in the second edition of Ingrid Jonker's *Versamelde werke,* edited by Abraham de Vries and published in Johannesburg in 1983.

84   NELM, Cope papers, Jack Cope diary, 5 November 1960.

85   Van Wyk, *Gesig van die liefde,* p. 56.

86   Van Wyk, *Gesig van die liefde,* p. 60.

87   NELM, Cope papers, Jack Cope diary, 14 July 1961.

88   Erna Sadie, *Ingrid Jonker: 'n Monografie* (thesis, University of Natal, 1978), p. 425.

89   Metelerkamp, *Ingrid Jonker,* pp. 115–17.

90   See Van der Merwe, *Gesprekke oor Ingrid Jonker,* pp. 193–9.

91   Interview with Aletta Greyling, in Ingrid Jonker, *Versamelde werke* (Johannesburg, 1983), p. 213.

92   Stellenbosch University Library, Krige papers, Bonnie Davidtsz to Uys Krige, 6 May 1964.

93   Brink, *A fork in the road,* p. 92.

94   Interview with Brink, 13 February 2012.

95   Shown in Nogueira, *Ingrid Jonker.* Cope also wrote about Ingrid having herself admitted to Valkenburg in his diary on 22 & 23 April 1962 (NELM, Cope papers).

96   Jack Cope, *The adversary within: Dissident writers in Afrikaans* (Cape Town, 1982), p. 82.

97   Jack Cope, 'A crown of wild olive', in Rabie (ed.), *In memoriam Ingrid Jonker*, p. 15.

98   Told by Amanda Botha, who heard Bertha Smit say this.

99   Information gleaned from NELM's summary of the documents currently with Gerrit Komrij and from the doctoral thesis of Johan van Wyk, who had access to the documents while they were still at NELM in the 1980s.

100   Peter McDonald, *The literature police: Apartheid censorship and its cultural consequences* (Oxford, 2009), p. 34.

101   Rabie, *Jan Rabie: Sestigers in woord en beeld*, p. 28; Cope, *The adversary within*, p. 85.

102   McDonald, *The literature police*, p. 171.

103   Metelerkamp, *Ingrid Jonker*, pp. 130–1.

104   Ingrid Jonker, *Versamelde werke* (Johannesburg, 1975), p. 229.

105   André Brink, in Van Schaik, *Korreltjie niks is my dood*.

106   Brink, *A fork in the road*, p. 102.

107   André Brink, in Nogueira, *Ingrid Jonker*.

108   Brink, *A fork in the road*, p. 103.

109   Brink, *A fork in the road*, p. 93.

110   Michael Cope, *Intricacy*, pp. 209–10.

111   Amanda Botha, 'Berta Smit: Miskende Sestiger, miskende digter?', 28 April 2010, www.versindaba.co.za/2010/04/28/berta-smit-miskende-sestiger-miskende-digter [accessed 23 August 2011].

112   Metelerkamp, *Ingrid Jonker*, p. 29.

113   Metelerkamp, *Ingrid Jonker*, p. 102.

114   Van Wyk, *Gesig van die liefde*, pp. 54–5.

115   McDonald, *The literature police*, pp. 95–6.

116   Bartho Smit, *Bartho Smit: Sestigers in woord en beeld* (Johannesburg, 1984), pp. 61–3.

117   Cope, *The adversary within*, pp. 86–7.

118   See Ingrid Jonker, *Versamelde werke* (Johannesburg, 1983), p. 213.

119   Quoted by Brink in Van der Merwe, *Gesprekke oor Ingrid Jonker*, pp. 254–5.

120   J.C. Kannemeyer, 'Feite onjuis, onvolledig', *Beeld*, 16 January 1987.

121   Metelerkamp, *Ingrid Jonker*, p. 135.

122 NELM, Cope papers, Jack Cope diary, 27 April 1964.

123 Stellenbosch University Library, Manuscript Section, Rabie papers, Ingrid Jonker to Jan Rabie & Marjorie Wallace, 14 June 1964.

124 Much of the information in the following paragraphs comes from Van Wyk, *Gesig van die liefde,* pp. 61–75.

125 NELM, Cope papers, Jack Cope diary, 12 June 1964.

126 Johan van Wyk, *Die dood, die minnaar en die oedipale struktuur in die Ingrid Jonker-teks* (PhD, Rhodes University, 1986), p. 110.

127 Augusta van Greunen, 'Liefdesdriehoek het haar alleen, beangs gelos', *Rapport,* 5 June 1994.

128 Told by Evalda Matthews in Nogueira, *Ingrid Jonker.*

129 Metelerkamp, *Ingrid Jonker,* p. 153.

130 See Van Wyk, *Gesig van die liefde,* p. 75.

131 Van Wyk, *Die dood, die minnaar en die oedipale struktuur in die Ingrid Jonker-teks,* p. 114; Sadie, *Ingrid Jonker,* p. 305, indicates that the poem was written earlier.

132 Metelerkamp, *Ingrid Jonker,* p. 152.

133 Metelerkamp, *Ingrid Jonker,* p. 154.

134 Metelerkamp, *Ingrid Jonker,* pp. 156–7.

135 Brink, *A fork in the road,* p. 109.

136 See letters to Bonnie Davidtsz, in Metelerkamp, *Ingrid Jonker,* pp. 164–7.

137 Van Wyk, *Gesig van die liefde,* p. 81.

138 Ingrid Jonker, *Selected poems,* p. 60.

139 Ingrid Jonker, *Black butterflies,* pp. 126–7.

140 Metelerkamp, *Ingrid Jonker,* p. 176.

141 Metelerkamp, *Ingrid Jonker,* p. 171.

142 Janet Malcolm, *The silent woman: Sylvia Plath and Ted Hughes* (New York, 1995), p. 172.

143 Sadie, *Ingrid Jonker,* p. 404.

144 Brink, *A fork in the road,* p. 110.

145 Metelerkamp, *Ingrid Jonker,* p. 174.

146 Anna Jonker in Van der Merwe, *Gesprekke oor Ingrid Jonker,* pp. 178–9.

147 Van Wyk, *Gesig van die liefde,* p. 82.

148 Van Wyk, *Gesig van die liefde,* p. 83.

149 Metelerkamp, *Ingrid Jonker,* p. 178.

150 Metelerkamp, *Ingrid Jonker,* p. 170.

151 Letter to Jack, in Metelerkamp, *Ingrid Jonker,* p. 178.

152 Freda Linde, in Van der Merwe, *Gesprekke oor Ingrid Jonker*, p. 179.
153 Metelerkamp, *Ingrid Jonker*, p. 176
154 Van Wyk, *Gesig van die liefde*, p. 83.
155 Metelerkamp, *Ingrid Jonker*, p. 180.
156 NELM, Cope papers, Jack Cope diary, 26 May 1965.
157 Metelerkamp, *Ingrid Jonker*, p. 182.
158 Metelerkamp, *Ingrid Jonker*, p. 188.
159 Metelerkamp, *Ingrid Jonker*, p. 190.
160 Van der Merwe, *Gesprekke oor Ingrid Jonker*, p. 167.
161 Anna Jonker, in Van der Merwe, *Gesprekke oor Ingrid Jonker*, p. 26.
162 Freda Linde, in Van der Merwe, *Gesprekke oor Ingrid Jonker*, p. 136.
163 This volume forms part of the Cope Collection, NELM.
164 Metelerkamp, *Ingrid Jonker*, pp. 172 & 180.
165 J.C. Kannemeyer, *Jan Rabie: Prosapionier en politieke padwyser* (Cape Town, 2004), p. 332.
166 Metelerkamp, *Ingrid Jonker*, p. 184.
167 Louw, 'In my arms digby die Seine …', p. 21.
168 Metelerkamp, *Ingrid Jonker*, p. 192.
169 Metelerkamp, *Ingrid Jonker*, p. 197.
170 Metelerkamp, *Ingrid Jonker*, p. 194.
171 Marjorie Wallace said that Abraham Jonker's words were repeated to her by the shocked policeman who phoned him with the news of Ingrid's death; see Rautenbach, *'n Olyftak vir onse Ingrid*, p. 52.
172 Metelerkamp, *Ingrid Jonker*, p. 197.
173 Metelerkamp, *Ingrid Jonker*, p. 202.
174 I was told this by Marina le Roux, whose husband Jan was the teacher.
175 Anna Jonker, in Van der Merwe, *Gesprekke oor Ingrid Jonker*, p. 36.
176 Nogueira, *Ingrid Jonker*.
177 Metelerkamp, *Ingrid Jonker*, p. 223.
178 Documentary by Christo Gerlach, *Verdrinkte hande* (1995).
179 Norman Holland, *Literary suicide: A question of style*, http://www.clas.ufl.edu/users/nholland/online.htm#suicide [accessed 20 January 2012].
180 McDonald, *The literature police*, pp. 128–30.

181 Rive, *Writing black*, pp. 113–14.

182 Athol Fugard, *Mourning Jonker and Nakasa*,
     http://heritage.thetimes.co.za/memorials/ec/AtholFugard/article.
     aspx?id=608761.

183 J.D.F. Jones, *Storyteller: The many lives of Laurens J. van der Post*
     (London, 2001), p. 267.

184 Letter to Bonnie, in Metelerkamp, *Ingrid Jonker*, p. 166.

185 'Ingrid Jonker-trust in nuwe hande', *Volksblad*, 29 May 2001;
     Anna Jonker, 'Geskrifte oor Ingrid gesoek', *Rapport*, 15 October
     1989; Stephan Terreblanche, 'Perskor settles dispute on poet's
     royalties', *Sunday Times*, 27 May 1984.

186 M.M. Hacksley, 'Anna Jonker het van Brink se briewe vernietig',
     Die Burger, 7 June 1994.

187 Ryan Creswell, 'Museum says it's not to blame for damage',
     Sunday Times, 5 June 1994.

188 Herman Wasserman, 'Polemiek "verbouereer" digter', *Die Burger*
     6 January 2001, p. 2; Elkarien Fourie, *Die feministiese biografie
     toegespits op die Afrikaanse digter Ingrid Jonker* (PhD, University
     of Pretoria, 2003), p. 262.

189 See Cope's introduction to Ingrid Jonker, *Selected poems*, p. 6.

190 McDonald, *The literature police*, p. 96.

191 Johann Potgieter, 'The new Sestigers', *Weekend Argus*, 25
     September 1982.

192 For references to Pereyre and Horn, see Barend Toerien, 'Ingrid:
     nogeens en vir oulaas', *Beeld*, 16 August 1994.

193 Cope, *A crown of wild olive*, p. 17; NELM, Cope papers, Jack
     Cope diary, 9 February 1959.

194 See the poem 'Ma', in Antjie Krog's debut volume, *Dogter van
     Jefta* (Cape Town, 1970), p. 12.

195 Metelerkamp, *Ingrid Jonker*, p. 155.

196 See interviews with Berta Smit, André Brink and the psychiatrist
     in Van der Merwe, *Gesprekke oor Ingrid Jonker*.

197 Metelerkamp, *Ingrid Jonker*, p. 77.

198 Freda Linde in Van der Merwe, *Gesprekke oor Ingrid Jonker*, p.
     136.

199 Cope, *A crown of wild olive*, p. 18.

200 Brink in Van der Merwe, *Gesprekke oor Ingrid Jonker*, p. 249.

Index